OUT OF FRAME

OUT OF FRAME

Growing Up Where I Didn't Belong

Michael Gordon Bennett

727 Squared Entertainment

Copyright © 2026 by Michael Gordon Bennett
All rights reserved.

No part of this book may be reproduced, stored in a retrieval system, or transmitted in any form or by any means—electronic, mechanical, photocopying, recording, or otherwise—without prior written permission of the publisher, except for brief quotations in reviews.

Published by 727 Squared Entertainment
Los Angeles, California
www.727squaredent.com

First Edition

ISBN: 978-0-9864162-6-2 (Paperback)
ISBN: 978-0-9864162-7-9 (Hardcopy)

This is a work of nonfiction. Certain names, identifying details, and events have been altered for privacy. The views expressed are those of the author and do not necessarily reflect those of any organization or institution.

This publication includes all rights of reproduction and adaptation, including audio, film, television, and other media now known or hereafter devised.

Printed in the United States of America

AUTHOR'S NOTE

The first edition of this book was written nearly a decade ago and published under a different title: *7–10 Split: My Journey as America's Whitest Black Kid*. The events it recounts have not changed. What has changed is my understanding of how to tell this story—and why it still matters. Time and distance have clarified the throughline. This edition reflects that clarity. It is not a revision of history, but a refinement of perspective.

Shortly after the book was published, my mother was diagnosed with Alzheimer's disease. From that point until her passing in April 2021, I became her caregiver. During those years, my career in entertainment—and my work as an author—came to a halt. Her death occurred in the midst of the COVID pandemic, a period that left little room for re-engagement or public conversation around the book. This edition marks the first opportunity to return to the work with intention.

What follows is a memoir, not a social thesis. It is a record of childhood and adolescence as I experienced them—shaped by memory, emotion, and the partial understanding of a young person trying to make sense of the world. Dialogue has been reconstructed to capture the substance and emotional truth of those moments rather than serve as a verbatim record. Some names and identifying details have been altered in the interest of privacy.

This is not a comprehensive portrait of Black America, nor an argument about race, class, or identity. It is one story, rooted in a specific set of circumstances: a Black child raised largely outside of Black cultural spaces, moving through environments where belonging was sometimes assumed, sometimes questioned, and sometimes quietly withdrawn. Any broader meaning drawn from these experiences belongs to the reader.

I do not offer conclusions or prescriptions. I am not interested in telling anyone what this story should mean—only in telling it as honestly as I can. If it resonates, unsettles, or provokes reflection, that response is its own destination.

This memoir is an invitation to look—at childhood, at environment, at identity—and at how much of who we become is shaped not by what we choose, but by where we are placed, and what we are taught to see.

PROLOGUE

I didn't plan on going in. It had been three decades since my son was born, and he knew little of my former life; I had made sure of that. Time has a way of making those decisions feel permanent, yet I found myself there anyway, close enough to recognize exactly what I'd been avoiding.

The parking lot looked like every other bowling alley lot in America: sun-bleached asphalt and oil stains like old bruises, with rows of cars that said nothing about the lives inside them. Families, teenagers, men in work boots, a couple on a date—it could have been any day in any year. But it wasn't.

My hand hovered over the door, caught between instinct and retreat, as if stepping inside might cost me something I wasn't ready to give up. I told myself I'd just peek—just look—to satisfy the curiosity that had survived a long silence.

The moment I pulled the door open, the place announced itself. Pins cracked, machinery roared to life, and balls rolled with a weight that felt intentional. It wasn't background sound; it was a confrontation. My throat tightened and my stomach dipped as my skin went alert, my body reacting the way bodies do when they re-enter rooms they once depended on.

My throat tightened. My stomach dipped. My skin went alert. My body reacted the way bodies do when they enter rooms they once depended on.

Then the smell followed: lane oil, old carpet, the faint burn of machinery, and grease from the snack bar. There was the sharp scent of cleaning solution trying to disguise years of sweat, sugar, and beer. It wasn't pleasant, but it was familiar.

I stood just inside the entrance, not moving, letting the moment settle. A few feet away, a kid—eight or nine years old—ran toward the approach with a ball too heavy for his frame. He swung it like a wrecking ball and sent it careening down the lane where it drifted, kissed the gutter, and stayed alive by a thread before finally clipping a single pin on the far right. The kid threw both arms into the air as if he'd just won the U.S. Open.

His father clapped while his mother laughed and strangers smiled. The boy didn't care how it looked; he only cared that it moved—that something he sent into the world did exactly what he asked it to do. I watched him celebrate that one pin as if it were everything.

It struck me then—sharp and unwanted—that the first thing bowling ever gave me wasn't skill. It gave me a place where effort mattered, a place where the lane didn't change its mind about who you were. It was a world where a kid could step up, do the work, and be rewarded with something clean and measurable, even if life outside those doors was anything but.

I moved forward slowly, like I was entering a church I hadn't visited since childhood. The counter, the shoe racks, the vending machines, and the neon specials on the wall didn't matter; my eyes went where they always used to go. The lanes stretched out as they always had—long, narrow, and lit from above—each one a private world, a possibility, and a test.

I could feel the old instincts waking up. It wasn't nostalgia, but the quiet math of angles, the muscle memory of the approach, and the deep need for control disguised as a hobby. I didn't bowl that day. I didn't rent shoes or step onto the approach to pretend I was the same boy or the same man. I just stood there and let the place speak, because bowling didn't just take my time when I was young—it took my pain and gave it somewhere to go. For years, I didn't know the difference.

The last time I bowled—really bowled—wasn't ordinary. It happened during elite league play in a fifty-lane center, the kind of place where serious bowlers know exactly what they're watching when something special starts to unfold. I was on lanes three and four. By the ninth frame, everyone within ten lanes knew what was happening, as nine strikes in a row has a way of announcing itself without words. People drifted closer, quietly at first, positioning themselves behind the settee while pretending they weren't watching. I didn't look up. I couldn't. Looking up would have broken the spell.

As I stepped into the tenth frame, the noise around me disappeared. The nearby lanes went still, conversations stopped, and balls waited untouched in the returns. Fifty lanes shrank to two. Strike ten was clean; strike eleven was cleaner. I knew then I was somewhere else—locked into a place where the body obeys without question and the mind stays out of the way. It is a zone you don't enter so much as surrender to.

When I released the twelfth ball, I didn't hope or guess. I knew. The moment it crossed the foul line, the shot was already finished. I stood there staring down the lane as the pins exploded, white and violent against the back curtain. My chest tightened and tears gathered before I could stop them. I swallowed hard, holding myself still, and then I turned.

The place erupted. Amidst the applause and cheers, a crowd I hadn't noticed was now standing—smiling men and women, Black and white, strangers celebrating something they could see but perhaps not fully understand. A voice cut through the noise over the loudspeaker: *Michael Bennett on lanes three and four just bowled a three hundred. Congratulations.*

What none of them could have known was how much that moment cost me. They saw control, precision, and calm, but they couldn't see the years that led there. They didn't see the nights when bowling wasn't a pastime but a refuge, or the discipline it demanded when the rest of the world felt unpredictable and hostile. They didn't know how the lanes absorbed what I couldn't say out loud.

Even my parents didn't know how deeply I struggled. I learned early how to bury what hurt me—how to carry racism, isolation, and fear without letting any of it show. Bowling gave me a place to survive when I couldn't find footing anywhere else.

That game happened two months before my son was born. As I stood there soaking in the applause, I knew it was time to walk away after twenty years of burying my emotions. People imagine moments like that as energizing, something that makes you want more, but for me, it did the opposite. It told me I was finished. So, I walked away and I didn't go back.

I kept the ball—not a shiny house ball, but mine, drilled to fit my fingers precisely. It sat quietly in closets and garages like a witness through moves and life changes that would have justified letting it go. It was never displayed or honored; it was just present. Some people keep objects because they believe the object holds the memory, but sometimes you keep it because you're not ready to admit what it carried you through.

I kept that ball for thirty-five years. Then, in 2021—months after my mother passed away—I finally threw it into a dumpster. It wasn't a ceremony. I waited until I was alone and opened the bag, which was actually older than the ball itself. I looked at it longer than I meant to, keeping silent so as not to turn the moment into something it didn't want to be. I lifted the ball, its weight surprising me as if it had been storing time, and then I let it go. It landed with a dull, final thud. No echo. No applause. Just silence.

Standing there, I understood what I hadn't as a boy: the things that save you can also keep you split. I wasn't born divided; that came later—slowly at first, then all at once. As a child, I moved through the world whole, curious, and unburdened by the meanings adults attach to skin, history, and expectation. I didn't question where I belonged because belonging had never been withheld from me.

The split came quietly, born from living inside a system that protected me while failing to prepare me. It came from learning how to function without naming what hurt, and from being praised for adaptability while never being taught what I was adapting to. Bowling didn't create the divide; it just gave me somewhere to put it.

On the lane, everything was aligned. The approach, the release, and the follow-through each belonged to the same motion. Outside the lane, nothing lined up that cleanly. I learned early how to compartmentalize, separating what I felt from what I showed and moving forward even when I didn't understand the rules of the game I was being asked to play.

That's what a 7–10 split is: two pins standing at opposite corners, demanding precision, control, and luck to clear them both. Miss one, and the frame is over; hit neither, and the failure is obvious. Every bowler knows it's one of the hardest shots in the game—not because it's impossible, but because it requires you to be exact under pressure.

That became my life, learning how to exist between two truths, two identities, and two worlds that didn't acknowledge each other, much less make room for overlap. I learned to aim carefully and adjust constantly, accepting that perfection was rare and mistakes were punished unevenly. I didn't know any of that then; I only knew how to keep rolling.

What complicates this story is not just what I learned later, but what I didn't know at all. When my family returned to the United States from Spain—just weeks before my eighth birthday—I carried none of the language, context, or warnings that might have helped me understand the country I was re-entering. I hadn't heard the names that shaped the decade or seen the images that unsettled the nation. I didn't know why some conversations stopped when I entered the room.

That ignorance wasn't accidental. It was the result of growing up inside a world that insulated its children from the fractures outside its gates, and of parents who, for reasons I wouldn't understand until much later, never filled in the gaps. I would spend years learning what I should have been taught long before, at the cost of the youthful exuberance I observed in everyone else.

ACT I
BEFORE THE CRACK

Chapter One

Powerful jet engines roared to life, and with a sudden surge, we were pressed back into our seats. We raced down the runway before lifting into the night sky, the plane angling east as the landing gear folded beneath us. Below, the lights of New York and New Jersey thinned and then vanished into the cloud cover.

Within minutes, there was nothing outside the window but darkness. My head stayed on a swivel—one moment watching the blinking lights at the wingtips, the next tracking flight attendants as they moved briskly through the aisle with trays of food. Anyone paying attention would have known immediately that this was my first time on an airplane.

My mother was only twenty-three, traveling alone with two small children—a five-year-old and a three-year-old—headed for a country we knew nothing about. That reality frightened her. Only years later did I learn she had an intense fear of flying, but at the time, all I knew was that the man she loved would be waiting for us at the other end of the journey.

Even at five, I could read her face. When I sensed her anxiety, I did what I did best: I talked. Constantly. The more she told me to be quiet, the more I filled the space, until eventually her tension softened and she finally rested.

After the cabin lights dimmed, sleep settled unevenly across the plane. My sister, Karen, and my mother drifted off quickly, but I stayed awake longer, staring into the blackness and searching for stars that never appeared. When I finally slept, it was brief.

Sunlight woke me.

Madrid was six hours ahead of New York, and morning had already begun by the time we descended. The ground rose fast as pressure filled my ears and the world's sound dulled into something distant. The plane struck the runway hard, snapping my head forward before the brakes screamed and the wings shuddered. Suddenly, we were standing in line at Spanish customs, surrounded by a language I didn't understand but immediately liked; it sounded expressive, full of movement and emotion.

Suddenly, we were standing in line at Spanish customs, surrounded by a language I didn't understand but immediately liked. It sounded expressive—full of movement and emotion.

Through a glass partition, I spotted my father.

It had been nearly a year since we'd seen him, yet he looked just like his pictures: strong, relaxed, and unmistakably present. He had arrived a month earlier, transferred from Morocco to Torrejón Air Base just outside Madrid. We embraced amid the noise of baggage claim, our exhaustion forgotten, and soon boarded a bus bound for Torrejón, where we would stay until our apartment in the city was ready.

Warm air poured through the open bus windows as we drove. My father narrated what passed outside, pointing out landmarks as though introducing us to a life already in motion. We stopped briefly at the hospital where he worked as an administrator—a place I would return to the following year to have my tonsils removed, though at the time it was just another building along the way.

The next morning, he hired a driver to take us sightseeing. We saw the Puerta de Alcalá, the Royal Palace, and the Plaza Mayor. I didn't grasp the history of what I was seeing; I only knew the city felt vast and welcoming in a way I had never experienced.

Our new home was a second-floor apartment in a ten-story building across from a park. The *Portero*—the building's doorman and superintendent—was a jovial, rotund man who spoke beautiful English, albeit with a thick Spanish accent. He greeted us warmly and showed us upstairs to a floor where military families, expatriates, and *Madrileños* lived side by side. Karen and I ran through the apartment until my father's voice stopped us cold; when he spoke like that, you listened.

The building wrapped around a central courtyard strung with clotheslines that ran on pulleys between the windows. I leaned out and looked up to see laundry fluttering everywhere—ordinary, communal, and entirely unfamiliar. Our neighborhood was busy and dense, filled with *mercados*, restaurants, and narrow streets crowded with people.

Within a week, Consuelo joined our household as a live-in maid. She walked me to school when my mother couldn't, took me to the markets, and taught me Spanish along the way. She was young, energetic, and affectionate, balancing discipline with a natural warmth.

I started kindergarten at Royal Oaks Elementary School two weeks after arriving. It was the first time I'd been away from my mother for more than a few hours, but I adjusted without trouble. Royal Oaks served American children from kindergarten through high school, creating a small, familiar pocket inside a foreign city.

Life moved easily—until November 22, 1963.

I didn't know the exact time President John F. Kennedy was assassinated; I only knew that Madrid grew quiet in a way I had never heard before. Spaniards gathered around radios and small black-and-white televisions as the streets emptied. The silence lingered. The *Portero* hugged every American who passed through the lobby, his eyes swollen and his shirt damp with tears.

The next morning, even the traffic seemed to pause. Wind moved dust across the park, lifting it briefly before letting it settle again. I watched, absorbing the stillness without understanding its cause. Consuelo took me to the *mercados*, where shopkeepers greeted us with solemn faces and unexpected generosity—free candy, soda, and small gestures offered without explanation. I felt the sadness around me, but at five, the loss of a president was abstract. What I understood instead was kindness.

My father came home late that night. I felt my bedroom door open just enough for him to look in, but I pretended to sleep. He closed it quietly and left again, not returning for days. Only later would I learn the military had been placed on high alert.

School felt different afterward. Teachers were tense and distracted, and even then, I noticed. They eventually succeeded in restoring normalcy, but Christmas break couldn't come soon enough. By spring, the city had resumed its usual pace.

During *siesta*—the long afternoon pause when much of Madrid shut down—I wandered farther than I should have, exploring streets until I lost my way and had to rely on strangers to point me home. I never felt afraid.

My father thrived there. He loved the nightlife, the music, the pace. Some evenings he took me along, setting me up at an outdoor table with peanuts, soda, and candy while he disappeared inside nearby bars.

My father thrived there. He loved the nightlife, the music, and the tempo of the city. Some evenings he took me along, setting me up at an outdoor table with peanuts, soda, and candy while he disappeared into nearby bars.

One might question why a father would leave his young child alone on the streets of a foreign city, and in hindsight, I have. But Madrid felt safe, the streets were familiar, and people watched out for one another. I never felt abandoned; I felt trusted. It didn't register as danger; it felt like freedom.

Flamenco dancers performed in the streets, sometimes pulling me into their routines, teaching me steps I didn't understand but followed anyway. I belonged everywhere.

That's why the news, when it finally came, felt unreal.

Orders arrived in the fall of 1965: we were leaving Spain. My father had been reassigned to Loring Air Force Base in northern Maine, just miles from the Canadian border. I didn't know what it meant—only that something good was ending.

On our last day, my father insisted Consuelo accept the money he pressed into her hands. She resisted at first, then broke down, holding on to him and crying openly. I stood there watching, my chest tight and my eyes burning. To me, Consuelo wasn't a maid; she was my constant, my translator, and my companion. I didn't understand then what it meant to lose someone who made the world feel navigable.

As if Spain itself objected to our departure, our plane was already racing down the runway when the pilot slammed on the brakes, throwing us forward in our seats. Armed security boarded and removed a man who had smuggled a small dog onto the flight.

My mother nearly passed out. She was almost eight months pregnant with my youngest sister, and doctors had tried in vain to get her to stay in Spain until after the birth. She had given them an emphatic "no"—a smart move, since she didn't speak the language—but that sudden stop on the runway nearly changed her mind.

Decades later, Mom admitted she was hesitant to come home. She knew just enough about what was happening in America to sense trouble ahead, especially for me. After many late-night conversations with my father, she had convinced herself that Maine was far away from the danger.

Chapter Two

The Man Before the Father. My father entered the world without a father of his own. Born in Baltimore in 1939 to a fifteen-year-old mother, his birth certificate left the line marked *Father's Name* blank; it simply read: *Baby Lee.* From the beginning, his existence carried a quiet stigma—one reinforced by the way questions were avoided and answers withheld.

He asked about his father when he was young. He pressed again as he got older, but each time the silence only hardened.

Not only did his mother take the secret to her grave, but so did the grandfather he idolized, along with most of his mother's siblings and cousins. No one ever broke ranks. No one ever explained. Over time, the questions stopped, but the absence remained—a permanent gap in his sense of self and an unanswered origin that followed him for the rest of his life.

Years later, it would be revealed that members of his family had considered terminating the pregnancy, an idea halted only by his grandfather's defiant intervention. That single act of protection became one of the few certainties my father carried forward: the knowledge that someone, at least once, had insisted he should exist.

After his aunt Sue adopted him and changed his last name to Bennett, his life gained a measure of stability, though it still lacked direction. He was raised by a succession of women—distant relatives who did what they could but were never positioned to teach a boy how to become a man. With no male role model to emulate, or steady paternal presence to absorb, much of his upbringing unfolded in bars owned by women by the women who raised him in Philadelphia and Atlantic City. They provided shelter and food but offered little guidance on tenderness or emotional availability. What he learned instead was toughness, self-reliance, and the ability to keep moving without complaint.

My father was light-skinned—what some in the Black community derisively called *high-yellow*. It was a label meant to diminish and question his authenticity, implying that his proximity to whiteness was a kind of betrayal. He endured years of contempt from both sides, too light for one world and never fully accepted in the other. While some Black people assumed he was white, some white people couldn't reconcile how he later married a Black woman. He learned early that visibility was not the same as belonging.

Before the Air Force provided him with structure, life offered few opportunities for upward mobility. He worked wherever he could, including a stint as a caddie at a whites-only golf course in Pleasantville, just outside Atlantic City. It was a place where women weren't allowed and where men spoke freely in his presence—unguarded, cruel, and confident that no one would challenge them. Years later, the stories he told me about what he overheard there made my blood pressure boil: the casual racism, open contempt and the absolute certainty that the world belonged to them and always would.

Everything began to change when he met my mother. Her father—my grandfather—treated my dad like a son from the moment they met. There was no hesitation, no hierarchy. For the first time in his life, my father experienced what it meant to be claimed by a man and he never forgot it. Even decades later, he spoke of my grandfather with a reverence reserved for someone who had given him something essential.

The military gave him rules, and my mother gave him softness. Between the two, he did the best he could. Sometimes that was enough; sometimes it wasn't.

* * *

The Woman Who Knew but Didn't Say would be a perfect title of a book to describe my mother. She grew up inside a different kind of silence, raised in a predominantly Black neighborhood in Atlantic City at a time when segregation was enforced openly and accepted quietly. She knew exactly where she was allowed to go and learned those boundaries early, adjusting to them without ceremony.

To her, Chicken Bone Beach wasn't an injustice; it was simply geography. It was the only beach open to Blacks, a fact that was known and accommodated, and rarely discussed. Segregation existed in her childhood the way the weather does—unavoidable, inconvenient, and not worth narrating once you've learned how to live around it.

Unlike my father, my mother wasn't shaped by chaos, but by restraint. She was observant, inward, and deeply intelligent. Books were her refuge and she read constantly, often juggling several at once and absorbing information without announcing what she carried. When she spoke, her words were usually measured and precise.

Despite her love of reading, she admitted to being a mediocre student with few career aspirations after high school. Any lingering professional pursuits changed the moment I entered the world, as she was a month pregnant with me before her graduation.

She loved deeply, but privately. Where my father confronted the world head-on, my mother endured it quietly. Where he demanded order, she practiced patience. She believed stability could be built through routine and protection—that if a child was loved and sheltered, the rest of the world could be handled later. To her, silence wasn't avoidance; it was insulation.

Together, my parents created a home that was loving, structured, and difficult to read. Discipline was immediate and rarely debated. We all understood the patriarchy of our family;

when my father spoke in a certain tone, my body reacted before my mind could catch up. I learned to stop moving, to listen closely, and to anticipate what was expected of me without ever asking why.

Punishment didn't always come with explanation. Sometimes it followed behavior I understood, while other times it arrived without warning, to correct something before it had a chance to grow. The rules were clear, even if their origins were not.

My mother softened what she could, quietly feeding me after I'd been sent to bed without dinner, choosing comfort over confrontation. But she rarely challenged my father directly. Peace in the house depended on balance, and balance depended on restraint.

So, I learned restraint. I learned when to speak and when to disappear. I learned to read posture, tone, and silence. I learned that asking *why* often made things worse, not better. No one told me this outright; I learned it simply by watching.

* * *

By the time we left Spain, the inheritance was already in place. I hadn't inherited my parents' pain directly, but I inherited their methods—their coping strategies, their reliance on control, routine, and silence as protection against a world that remained largely unnamed.

I was loved. I was protected. I was disciplined.

But I was not prepared. No one explained what lay ahead or why preparation mattered. The world was something to be handled later, when I was older, when the time was right. At the time, that felt like safety. Only later would I understand what that safety had cost.

Chapter Three

November 1965

We arrived at Loring Air Force Base just before Thanksgiving. A stiff wind shot through the door of our temporary quarters the moment it opened—sharp and immediate, as if winter had been waiting for us.

Loring sat in the northeastern corner of Maine, near a town called Limestone. On a windy day, I could have thrown a snowball from my bedroom window and landed it near the Canadian border.

Interstate 95 ended sixty miles south in Houlton before bending toward Canada, and Presque Isle—the nearest town of consequence—was twenty-five miles away and barely cracked ten thousand residents.

Snow accumulated in feet, not inches. Paths mattered; stray from them and you risked sinking chest-deep into drifts hardened by wind and ice. Sometimes, the sun glistening off the snow was blinding.

The cold didn't ease in; it asserted itself. Bare hands burned, breath crystallized, and paint peeled from buildings that looked like they'd been standing at attention too long.

While the temperature hovered in the upper twenties, the wind chill often drove them into single digits. A persistent coat of snow claimed the ground from September through May, rendering the world a slick, unfamiliar landscape.

Spain had ended—but not cleanly. Emotionally, none of us had truly arrived because Spain hadn't released us yet. The contrast was immediate and unforgiving. Madrid had been warmth and sound, late nights, and open windows, with music drifting through streets that stayed alive well past dark.

Loring was cold, rigid, sealed tight against the elements. Doors closed quickly here, windows stayed shut, and silence pressed in early. The vibrant, energetic language I'd grown accustomed to warm suddenly replaced by one that felt dull, lacking in both rhythm and charm.

We ate Thanksgiving dinner at the NCO Club and two weeks later, we moved into our new home on Foulouis Drive. Fifteen days after that, my sister Amanda was born, arriving just one day after my mother's birthday.

I ignored my Christmas gifts and sat by her bassinet for hours, marveling at how something so small could exist so quietly. When Mom placed her in my arms, she fidgeted briefly and then returned to sleep. I'd never held a baby before; much later, I'd joke that I dropped her on her head claiming it was the only way to explain her stubbornness.

It struck me later what the odds must have been: two Black girls born in Maine, at opposite ends of the state six years apart. My sister Karen was born in Kittery, Maine, while we were stationed at Pease Air Force Base in New Hampshire; because that base had nothing more than a clinic, we were forced to the Navy base across the border.

Dad didn't say much about our new environment during those first few months, but I could feel his sense of loss. He moved through our new house like a man who had left something behind. The music he played told the story better than words—Spanish records spinning on our turntable, names I didn't recognize, and rhythms that didn't belong to this place. It was as if he were trying to keep Madrid alive indoors, one song at a time.

Most of the responsibility for settling us fell on Dad. Mom's pregnancy combined with the fact she didn't drive, limited her mobility and placed a burden on him that extended long past Christmas. He did it without complaint, but you could see the exhaustion written all over him.

With a precision that would make a marching band proud, he started his new assignment, registered two kids for school, bought winter clothing for a cold we were forced to respect, find a doctor for Mom, secure furniture, shopped for Christmas, and move us into permanent housing.

I started second grade at Harrison Elementary a week after arriving. My fear of the new surroundings evaporated quickly and friends came easily. We were military kids—bright, adaptable, and still largely innocent.

Walking to and from school in those winter months was always an adventure. The sun appeared on the eastern horizon just after 7 a.m., only to disappear by 3:30 p.m. At first, the trek was brutal. My face burned even under the protection of a mask and my fingers ached inside thick gloves that never quite did their job. But like everything else, I adapted—helped along by classmates who treated the bitter cold as a routine rather than a hardship.

Chapter Four

Winter settled into Loring with a kind of stubborn authority. Snow didn't just fall; it accumulated, piling into drifts that swallowed familiar shapes whole. Cars disappeared for days at a time as plows and snowblowers carved narrow corridors through the streets, heaving white walls of snow onto garage rooftops just to keep the roads passable.

It became a ritual. Dad eventually gave up on the garage entirely, parking our Cadillac on the street, though that offered little protection. Even with an orange scuba-diving flag attached to the antenna, the car routinely vanished beneath fresh layers of snow. More than once, I watched neighbors wander the street with broom handles, poking blindly into snowbanks and listening for the dull thud that meant they'd found a buried vehicle.

One winter storm was so relentless we couldn't open either door to the house. Dad and I had to climb out through an upstairs window and took turns shoveling downward, hour after hour, until we finally reached the front porch. By then, the snow had frozen solid, and we had to chip it away with an ice pick just to get back inside. I was nine years old, exhausted, every muscle screaming; I slept that night like I'd been hit with a tranquilizer.

That Christmas, I received the most prized gift of my childhood—a white telescope with a black eyepiece. It wasn't the Palomar Observatory, but in my mind it might as well have been. I guarded it like my life depended on it.

Our living room window was wide and mostly unobstructed, the perfect vantage point. So I planted the telescope there and waited impatiently for nightfall. On evenings when frost or ice crystallized across the glass, I grabbed an ice scraper and went outside to clear my view. My parents thought I'd lost my mind. I didn't care.

At the time, it never occurred to me that the moon wasn't always visible. On evenings when it decided to take up residence over some other part of the Earth, I grew petulant, convinced it had personally betrayed me.

Somewhere along the way, a fascination with space took hold. Whether it started in school or was sparked by the constant drumbeat of the Space Race I was hooked. Dad and I tracked craters and constellations, matching what I saw through the lens to diagrams in my book: the Little Dipper, the Big Dipper and Polaris—the North Star. Years later, during the Apollo 11 landing, I still wouldn't let the movers touch that telescope.

Baseball came later—in the spring, not the winter. We had only a handful of television channels—NBC, CBS, and PBS—. And the only team we ever saw was the Boston Red Sox. Every kid I knew played baseball, lived it and breathed it. By the time I turned ten, I'd become a full-fledged baseball historian, memorizing stats and lineups, and reading encyclopedias under the covers with a flashlight long after I was supposed to be asleep.

But winter had forced me indoors long before baseball claimed me and that's when I picked up a habit both my parents loved: reading. Books became my refuge and third-grade readers turned into doorways I didn't yet know how to name. My teacher, Mrs. Tweetie—and yes, that was her real name—once asked me to read a passage from a play aloud to the class.

I was terrified at first, but then something strange happened. Without thinking, I started giving each character a different voice. Fifteen minutes passed; no one interrupted and no one laughed. When I finished, the class clapped. Where the bravado came from was a mystery, but what mattered was the sensation of something finally unlocking.

As for Spain, it had begun to fade. Nearly a year had passed without speaking a word of Spanish to anyone but Dad, who occasionally tested me just to see what remained. The language returned in fragments, then slipped away again.

Spain resurfaced only when he played his new Spanish-language albums, the music drifting through our house like a visitor who refused to announce himself. To this day, I don't know how he kept receiving new Spanish music. I can only assume they came from one of the many Spanish friends we left behind.

Chapter Five

Nothing announced itself at first. Life on base still ran with the precision I'd come to expect; reveille came and went, School bells rang on time, streets were cleared, and rules were enforced. Adults wore uniforms that made authority easy to read and there was a deep comfort in that. Order felt permanent.

Even our house carried it. Like every home on the block, a metal sign was bolted to the front door—black letters on a yellow background—bearing my father's rank and name:

SSGT R.L. BENNETT

Authority wasn't merely suggested; it was posted. If something in the world was broken, I assumed someone older would explain it. They always had—until they didn't.

At first, the change was subtle. It wasn't insults or threats, but rather moments that ended too quickly: conversations that shifted when I entered the room or rules that seemed to bend without explanation. I noticed them the way kids do, instinctively, without knowing what to call them. Something felt off, but nothing had happened yet.

On base, fairness felt automatic, but outside the gates, it felt conditional. I didn't have language for that difference—only the sense that the farther you moved from military order, the less predictable the world became. Still, life went on. Between homework, dinner and the television humming in the background, no one sat me down to explain what lay beyond the perimeter fence. No one warned me that the rules could change depending on where you stood—or who you were.

So, I adjusted. I watched more and talked less. I paid attention to tone and timing, noting the way a laugh could land wrong and hang in the air longer than it should. I didn't feel afraid. I felt alert.

The crack finally showed itself on an ordinary afternoon. I was at a friend's house, sitting cross-legged on the floor with army men scattered between us, lost in a battle we'd invented. We'd just come back from Cub Scouts, still in our blue uniforms, buzzing about an upcoming camping trip to the Maine woods. We talked about canoe rides and roasting marshmallows, comparing merit badges and showing off brand-new pocketknives, laying them carefully on the carpet like trophies, while Cub Scout insignia catching the light.

Outside, the early evening dimmed. The television played in the background—noise more than content—until suddenly, it wasn't. A breaking news bulletin flashed across the screen. My friend's father rushed into the room and turned up the volume, nearly stepping on his son in his haste.

"It's about time someone killed that nigger."

The word landed before I could catch it. I'd never heard it before, but I knew instantly who it was meant for. Whatever venom targeted the man on the screen reached me too. If he hated that Black man, what did that make me?

The room changed. The air felt heavier and I froze where I sat, suddenly aware of my body in a way I never had been. I didn't cry and I didn't speak; I simply I waited. My friend's mother moved fast—too fast. She grabbed my coat, guided me toward the door, and hugged me tighter than necessary. She whispered that everything would be okay.

Okay from what?

I ran home as fast as my ten-year-old legs would carry me, the cold biting through my open jacket. By the time I reached our house, the sky had gone dark.

Inside, my mother's eyes were red, she had just hung up the phone with my father. The television showed the same images on repeat until Mom finally turned it off, trying to protect me. A question formed in my mind about what the word meant—but something stopped me from asking it then.

I ate dinner quietly and went to my room to read baseball books, but word followed me anyway.

The next day at school was worse—not because anyone said anything, but because people knew things I didn't. Teachers were tense and classmates whispered. Until then, the man who had been killed was a stranger to me and that ignorance felt unbearable. That afternoon, I went straight to my mother.

"Who was he?" I asked. She explained carefully while she cooked dinner. Later, when my father came home, he changed into a suit for his second job and sat down to eat. It felt like the only moment I'd get.

"What does nigger mean?" I asked.

The room went silent. Dad's face turned a shade of red I'd never seen, his eyes were cold.

"Where'd you hear that word?"

I told him everything. To his credit, he stayed. He explained slowly, honestly, even though it made him late for work that night. Then his calm turned to anger—not loud, but focused and dangerous.

"How dare he say that around my son."

That was the first time I saw rage aimed outward on my behalf and it wouldn't be the last time I heard the word in the days to follow. The crack was no longer invisible. Once you hear it, you can't unhear it. It wasn't just the word; it was the venomous intent, imparted by the tone of my friend's father, that sat with me for days on end.

Chapter Six

The name followed me home. It stayed with me long after the explanations ended, appearing everywhere: on the radio, on television, and in classrooms where adults spoke with a care that bordered on fragile. They said his name softly, as if volume alone might disturb something precarious.

Martin Luther King Jr.

What unsettled me wasn't knowing his name; it was the realization of how easily everyone else seemed to have known it all along.

My fourth-grade teacher was a Black woman married to a service member, and under normal circumstances, she ran her classroom with a calm, practiced authority. But that Friday, she was different. I remember the uncharacteristic hesitation in her voice, and the way she paused longer than necessary before answering even simple questions. A pained expression surfaced and receded across her face as if every sentence required a private negotiation before it could be spoken aloud.

She stood before twenty-five students—about a third of us Black, the rest white—and tried to proceed as if nothing extraordinary had happened. I can see now how narrow that path must have been for her. She had to acknowledge without provoking it; she had to maintain order without pretending the world wasn't shifting outside our windows. Even then, without fully understanding the "why" of it, the strain was unmistakable. She wasn't just teaching us that day' she was holding the room together.

Some students asked questions that revealed how much they already understood, while others simply stayed quiet, watching. I was one of the watchers.

I felt exposed—not necessarily because of my own ignorance, but because I hadn't known I supposed to be anything other than a child. History had been unfolding while I was looking elsewhere, and I suddenly had a lifetime of catching up to do.

At home, the television was almost always tuned to the news, and the images of Vietnam filled our living room most nights. I would absorb fragments of the conflict until I was eventually sent away so my father could watch in peace. Yet strangely, I have no memory of the Civil Rights Movement from that time. It must have been there—it had to have been—but I had missed it completely.

We had a newspaper delivered every day and my ritual was always the same: I'd bring it inside, tear out the sports section, and neatly put the rest back together for my father. The front page never held my attention; I only cared about the box scores.

Learning Dr. King's name didn't clarify the world for me; it complicated it. It revealed that the reality I thought I understood had been operating on terms that were never made visible to me. My innocence didn't vanish all at once that week, but the assumption that the world would always explain itself did. And once that assumption is gone, you stop listening to what people say—and start paying attention to what they don't.

Chapter Seven

Within a few weeks of Dr. King's death, everything in my world appeared to return to normal. School resumed its rhythm, adults stopped lowering their voices, and the television returned to its usual rotation of Vietnam updates and weather reports. If Dr. King's name was mentioned at all, it was brief and offered without explanation. It was as if he had passed through my life and simply vanished.

My ten-year-old mind couldn't place April 4, 1968, anywhere it could make sense; I felt the shock and saw the reaction, but then watched it dissolve. There was no framework for it, no language that held. Life simply kept moving—and so, did I.

Bowling was part of that movement. My mother had taught me to bowl when I was seven and it became something we could do together during the long Maine winters—just the two of us. My father hated bowling, one sister was still an infant, and the other had no interest, so Bowling became our thing: uncomplicated and shared.

By the time I was nine, I joined a Saturday morning youth league. bowling every week at nine o'clock, winter after winter. There were no practices; you simply showed up, bowled, and went home. I liked it because it was fun, because it got me out of the house and because in a place where winter pressed in hard, it gave me something to look forward to.

After league play, if the weather cooperated and my mother was feeling generous, she would give me enough money to walk to the movie theater nearby. It showed double features—whatever had already been out long enough to stop being special—and I sat alone in the dark, watching whatever was playing and eating more candy than I should have.

Sundays followed their own rigid routine: church in the morning, Sunday school afterward. It was always the same pew, same hymns, the same cadence. Most military families didn't talk about politics, and race rarely entered the conversation unless it could be folded into something general, like service or charity.

Church never quite made sense to me and neither did Sunday school. My parents didn't attend—ever. They'd been married in the Catholic Church, and my mother agreed to raise us Catholic, but she never abandoned her African Methodist Episcopal roots, and my father never set foot inside beyond the threshold. I went because it was expected, standing and sitting when everyone else did, but the service felt distant, procedural.

Sunday school was even worse. The classes were usually taught by a parent with no real grounding in theology, who jumped from verse to verse in ways that even my ten-year-old mind could tell were selective. It felt less like teaching and more like steering toward conclusions I didn't yet understand but already resisted.

I don't remember what was said from the pulpit the Sunday after Dr. King died; I only remember standing for a moment of silence and the priest saying his name. That was all.

That summer, I played Little League baseball for the first time, and it took up a space in my life that was suddenly communal. The fields were busy from morning until dusk, filled with shouting parents, dust clouds, and the crack of a bat. My team was the Yankees. Playing for the Yankees in Red Sox country didn't win us many fans, but at ten years old, that hardly mattered—being on a team was enough.

Only days after Robert Kennedy was assassinated, we played a Saturday game that began with a moment of silence. I stood still like everyone else, but when it ended, the pause dissolved quickly. Gloves snapped, bats swung and boys laughed; youth reclaimed the afternoon.

Somewhere in the middle of the game, a white woman—whose son was on our team—shouted from the stands, "Strike that nigger out." The words rolled off her tongue as if they'd always been there. My teammate froze. Then he collapsed into tears, sobbing so hard he could barely breathe. The game stopped—not because of the rules, but because everyone felt the blow.

My father turned in the stands, anger flashing across his as he prepared to confront her, but my mother grabbed his arm hard enough to stop him. This wasn't his fight—not this time. A group of parents, Black and white, stepped in as the umpire halted the game. The woman was escorted from the field, but the damage was already done.

For weeks afterward, my teammate carried it with him. Kids avoided him, and neighborhood games went on without him. Even when school started, the distance remained. It was those of us who were Black who eventually pulled him back in—sitting with him, playing with him, and treating him like he still belonged. The tears on his face that day still haunt me.

On the drive home, my father launched into one of his rants about the word. The slur was never used in our house, not even as a sign of affection that so many Black Americans claim; in his eyes, it was a form of self-loathing.

He glanced at me in the rearview mirror. "If I ever hear you use—,"

"Richard!" Mom shouted, cutting him off.

I stayed quiet, staring out the window, replaying my teammate's face in my mind. How a parent could do something like that to their own child was beyond me. I only knew it hurt to watch.

Chapter Eight

JULY 1969

The last thing I saw before we pulled away wasn't the house itself, but a junior enlisted man standing at our front door. He unscrewed the metal nameplate, paused for a moment, and then handed it to my father. Dad turned it over in his hand like a keepsake, though neither of us said a word about keeping it. That simple exchange made our departure feel real; our time there would leave no trace. In a few days, another family would live behind that door, then another—every name replaced, every household temporary. In Maine, even your presence came with an expiration date.

It would take a few years, but every one of our neighbors would eventually, scattered to new bases across the globe. Loring Air Force Base would exist only in memory; by the mid-1990s, it would be closed, our house torn down. Only the streets would remain. I was old enough to understand that moves weren't vacations; they were endings disguised as beginnings.

We drove south on U.S. Highway 1, headed for Interstate 95. The road cut through dense forest—eastern white pines stacked like a wall on either side—interrupted by rivers that flashed silver through the trees. In the distance, mountains rose against the bright summer sky, their peaks still showing stubborn patches of snow, as if winter didn't fully believe in July. It struck me then how Maine could be breathtaking when it wasn't trying to kill you.

Four years earlier, I'd had no eyes for any of it—only cold, wind, and the strange quiet of a place so remote it felt like the end of the map. Now, as the wilderness slid past the windows like a farewell postcard, I felt a surge of gratitude. It wasn't love or nostalgia, but a simple recognition: the place had been real—hard, beautiful, and formative in ways I couldn't yet name.

Dad drove like he belonged on that highway, his hands steady and his posture alert. He didn't look like a man leaving anything behind; he looked like a man executing a plan. Six hours later, we pulled into Portsmouth, New Hampshire—Pease Air Force Base—one of the earliest chapters in our family's story. Dad's mood lifted the moment we crossed into familiar territory, and he slipped into tour-guide mode, pointing out landmarks as if confirming the memories were still there.

Mom sat quietly, smiling. New Hampshire had been the first place she ever lived outside Atlantic City, and those early years hadn't been easy. Dad was rarely home then, juggling multiple jobs alongside his Air Force duties just to keep food on the table. Military pay in the late fifties barely scraped the poverty line—an unspoken truth about service no one seemed eager to acknowledge.

"There," he said, as if the past might still be parked where he left it. "That's where we used to go."

He found our old house, the drive-in movie theater and the A&W we'd frequented back when I was too young to remember anything but the feeling of it. It was the old-school version, where a tray of food arrived and hooked onto your car door like it belonged there. Dad kept asking if I remembered. Of course I didn't—I was three when we left—but I didn't want to disappoint him on a day like that, so I offered him something truth-adjacent and harmless.

"I remember the smell," I said. It was partly true, but mostly the imagination of a boy trying to offer his father a gift he could accept. Dad smiled anyway, satisfied enough to keep moving.

The following morning, before continuing south, Dad detoured to a lighthouse overlooking the ocean. He'd been there years earlier with Karen and me when we were babies and now, he took us again, as if returning might stabilize something inside him. We sat on rock cliffs while the Atlantic roared below, waves slamming into jagged stone and exploding into mist that dampened our skin. For a moment, the horizon disappeared; then it returned, and a rainbow formed in the spray as casually as if the world offered beauty on schedule. The sound swallowed everything—conversation, thought, and the cry of seabirds overhead. It was the kind of roar that reminded you the planet didn't care what you were carrying in your chest.

By noon, Dad announced it was time to go. We had four hundred miles to cover—the distance to Atlantic City. Somewhere beneath our brief trip down memory lane, Vietnam rode with us. In less than three weeks, Dad would be gone. I didn't have the courage to say it out loud, but the questions lived inside me, persistent and unwelcome. *Would he come back injured? Would he come back at all?*

Dad was due for reassignment after four years in Maine, but he still hadn't been promoted. That failure sat in him like a burr—unspoken, ever-present. He understood how the system worked, and after many late-night conversations with Mom—voices low, doors closed— he had made a decision. He would volunteer. If he survived, there would be a promotion waiting. That was the bargain. I didn't know that then, not officially, but the walls in our house were thin and I was a light sleeper. At eleven, choosing danger made no sense to me, but I knew that whatever lay ahead wasn't optional; my father had already decided to meet it head-on.

The closer we got to New Jersey, the more the landscape softened into more towns, more traffic, and more signs of life outside the military bubble. Loring had trained me to accept isolation as normal, but the rest of the country hadn't. The stench of marshland announced our arrival on Absecon Island before any sign did, hitting my nose like a memory I didn't know I had—brackish water, mud, and salt.

Then the lights. Atlantic City glowed in the distance, brighter than anything I'd seen in years. My eyes locked on them the way they once had on Madrid. It wasn't the same kind of beauty, but it was the same sensation: the world was expanding.

Dad found WMID on the radio and cranked up the music—The Four Tops, The Temptations, Diana Ross and The Supremes, Stevie Wonder— as if the songs could drown out what he refused to say. He sang along, loud and confident, turning the car into his personal concert hall. He had a great voice; he'd missed his calling. When Mom joined in, their voices braided together, and for a few fleeting minutes, the space between us felt whole and almost joyful. For a little while, Vietnam couldn't get a word in.

We pulled up to 1307 Drexel Avenue after dark. The moment the door opened, the house spilled out love like it had been waiting for us the whole time—hugs, kisses, *my-mys* and *Lordy-lordys*, hands on cheeks and shoulders, arms reaching as if we might disappear if they didn't hold on long enough.

Granny was the first force I felt. She was small—under five feet—but her presence made height irrelevant. When she hugged me, pulling away felt like committing a sin. I didn't just feel welcomed; I felt claimed.

Grandpop stood behind her like a quiet foundation. Integrity radiated from him; from the way he held himself and the way he looked at all of us. I hadn't known it was possible to feel that safe inside another person's house.

After the initial storm of greetings, Dad steered us back into motion. We weren't staying on Drexel Avenue that night. We drove to Pleasantville, to a place I'd only seen in pictures: Cedar Inn. It sat back off Black Horse Pike, removed from the road by brush and evergreen trees. The marquee out front was shaped like a giant Christmas tree, trimmed in green lights with red lettering—an island of glow in the dark. Even quiet and closed, the place felt like it held stories in its walls.

For two weeks, we moved between Atlantic City and Pleasantville, between family warmth and the quiet moments when the future kept tapping me on the shoulder. Then August 16 arrived. We stood at the bus station and watched Dad board a Trailways bus bound for McGuire Air Force Base.

Next stop: Vietnam.

Mom and Dad held each other like they were trying to reverse time through contact alone. The driver had to hurry them along not understanding that the hug wasn't romance—it was survival. I tried to hold my face still, tried to keep my eyes dry, tried to be whatever kind of son I thought a man needs when he's about to walk into a war. I failed.

The tears came hot and fast. Dad looked at me—just a look—then climbed the steps. The door folded shut. We stood frozen as the bus pulled away, him waving through the window, holding back his own emotion. We didn't move until it was gone. Mom trembled beside me, her body shaking with a reality she could no longer postpone. Vietnam wasn't something on television now. It wasn't a rule about staying quiet during the news.

It had taken my father. And all the lights in Atlantic City couldn't change that.

Chapter Nine

AUGUST 1969

Black Horse Pike was a divided four-lane road, speed limit fifty-five and the traffic was constant and unforgiving. Cars and trucks tore past day and night, the roar of them never fully leaving you. Directly across the highway stood Storybook Land, a family theme park where bright signs and summer laughter drifted through the air—a strange, cheerful counterpoint to the world where we lived.

This was not a Black neighborhood. Most of the homes within a mile radius were white-owned and scattered far apart, separated by thick forest and long gravel driveways. It was rural and isolated, save for the highway cutting through the trees. Cedar Inn stood alone—a destination rather than a community.

The place belonged to my father's aunt, Ethel. She was in her sixties then: sharp, commanding, and tireless.

Long before we arrived, her family had owned Cedar Inn for decades. It had been founded during the era of segregation, when Black travelers and workers had limited options for food, drink, or lodging along major highways.

For years, the Inn had served as a refuge—a place where Black working-class men and women could gather without explanation or apology. By the time we moved in, it no longer operated as a hotel and the guest rooms sat empty, but the bar downstairs was very much alive.

The building rose three stories. The basement held the bar—a long wraparound counter, two pool tables, a jukebox, and a dance floor worn smooth by decades of feet. The second floor was a maze of old rooms, long closed and filled with mismatched furniture, stacked mattresses, and forgotten boxes.

It held a large formal dining room and a front sitting area from another era where we watched TV. The third floor was ours: three bedrooms and a single bathroom with a clawfoot tub that had survived more generations than I could imagine.

Less than a mile away sat the whites-only golf course where my father had caddied as a teenager. The proximity would strike me later. At the time, it simply meant that two very different worlds existed almost side by side—and never touched. This was my first sustained exposure to Black America outside the military.

The men who frequented Cedar Inn were blue-collar types with hands thick and calloused by years of construction, auto repair, and factory shifts. Few held white-collar jobs; many were the sons and grandsons of men who had sat at that same bar long before them. Their lives carried weight—financial strain, limited options, and little margin for error.

The women worked service jobs in restaurants, cleaning, or retail. Whatever disposable income they had often found its way here. Cedar Inn wasn't just a bar; it was continuity. Other than delivery drivers, I don't remember ever seeing a white person enter the place.

Sometimes, during quieter hours, I sat at the top of the stairs leading down to the bar—out of sight but close enough to hear. I listened to conversations I'd never heard before: talk of discriminatory bosses, bills, wives, and Philadelphia sports. There was a hardness to these lives I couldn't yet relate to, only register. Eventually, Aunt Ethel would discover me and send me back upstairs, but by then, the sounds had already settled in.

At night, from my bedroom window, I watched the other side of Cedar Inn come alive. On Fridays and Saturdays, drunken patrons spilled into the gravel lot. Some staggered; others argued. More than once, women arrived looking for husbands who hadn't come home. Voices rose, accusations flew, and I saw slaps land and men retreat. These scenes played out beneath my window like unscripted theater—raw, emotional, and unresolved.

During the day, Karen and I explored the empty second-floor rooms. In one of them, I stumbled across a seventh-grade paper my father had written years earlier. His handwriting was terrible—a trait that followed him for life—and the margins were filled with drawings and a barely disguised disdain for the nuns at his Catholic school. I smuggled the papers upstairs and shared them with Mom; we laughed for days, and she even mentioned it in a letter to Dad. I often wondered what his face looked like when he read that I'd uncovered a piece of his past he likely assumed was gone forever.

My sister and I were convinced Cedar Inn was haunted, and we had the evidence to prove it. The old wooden frame groaned and squealed at random hours, loud enough to stop you mid-step. Doors slammed shut without a draft or explanation, and floorboards complained even when no one was walking on them. At night, lying in bed, we listened to the building talk to itself and quietly agreed that this place had a past it wasn't finished sharing. We never told Aunt Ethel. She would've laughed us straight back upstairs.

Bowling remained part of my routine, but not in the way it had been in Maine. At Cedar Inn, loneliness was a constant companion. In Maine, I could walk outside and find friends, but here, school friendships rarely extended beyond the bus ride home. Once I was dropped off, the world narrowed quickly.

Every Saturday morning, I rode my bike two miles down Black Horse Pike to Northfield Lanes for junior league. My bowling bag hung from the handlebars, bumping against the frame as cars blasted past inches away. There was no bike lane, just a narrow shoulder and the knowledge that I didn't really belong there. But I went anyway.

Once or twice a week, I rode the Pike in the opposite direction to visit the only friend I saw outside of school that year, a boy I'll call Jim. His parents owned what amounted to the white equivalent of Cedar Inn in a neighboring town. I entered through a side door every time, passing white patrons who watched me with narrowed eyes, trying to decide what a Black kid was doing there. Jim's parents tolerated me, but Jim was never allowed to come my way. The friendship existed only on their terms, on their ground. After a month of these visits, I stopped going. Naive as I was, it was clear even then that something darker was at work in Jim's family—and in how they saw me.

That year also brought my first real crush. Her name was Kim—blonde, White, a tomboy in every sense of the word. Tough. Fearless. Sixth-grade eyes that hadn't yet learned their power. We talked easily at school. Everyone knew we liked each other.

That year also brought my first real crush. Her name was Kim—a blonde, fearless tomboy with sixth-grade eyes that hadn't yet learned their power. We talked easily at school, and everyone knew we liked each other. I never considered how our closeness might look to others, and neither did she. At that age, kids seemed less susceptible to race—or so it felt. But she lived in a world I couldn't follow her into; Cedar Inn made that much clear.

Between the bar downstairs, the isolation upstairs, and the bike rides along Black Horse Pike, a pattern was taking shape: my life didn't fit neatly anywhere. For the first time, I felt that gap beginning to widen.

Chapter Ten

The trouble didn't announce itself all at once; it arrived on schedule. Usually, it started the moment the school bus pulled up, though sometimes it waited until recess or lunch. Occasionally, it followed me all the way home. The pattern didn't matter as much as the consistency.

The attacks came from Black students, a fact that confused me at first. I stood out. I didn't belong to the neighborhood, and everyone knew my father was in Vietnam. That absence carried its own heavy meaning: it marked me as exposed. There was no father nearby to show up, no threat of immediate consequence, and no adult presence tied directly to me in that place. I hadn't grown up with these kids, and I hadn't earned my place among them; I had arrived already marked as "other."

To them, I looked like I had something they didn't. It wasn't money—we didn't have that—but I carried myself like someone who did. I had clean clothes, a full lunch, and books always in my hands. I was tall, articulate, and visibly comfortable in a classroom. My parents had drilled one message into me early: *do your best in school.* In that environment, my academic comfort translated as weakness, and jealousy found its opening there.

The goal wasn't just humiliation; it was pain. Rocks, batteries—anything hard enough to hurt and small enough to throw without consequence. The attacks weren't impulsive; they were ritualized, designed to remind me daily that being different came with a cost. Even high schoolers ventured over to inflict bodily harm.

My mother hated fighting and avoided it instinctively, using silence and patience as her tools. My father believed the opposite: any punch thrown in your direction had to be answered decisively and overwhelmingly. If I didn't fight back, he promised he would punish my inaction in ways I couldn't imagine.

I had seen his philosophy in action back in Maine. Two brothers, both several years older than me, had constantly beaten me with whatever objects they could find. One had even hit the back of my skull with a hammer, requiring a trip to the emergency room and six stitches. One day, while my father was home from work, those same brothers followed me and trapped me near our front door. Instead of intervening, Dad walked out, set up a lawn chair in the front yard, and sat down. He instructed me to fight back. I hesitated until he threatened to spank me for my cowardice.

I picked up a tree branch and caught one of the boys across the face, sending blood gushing everywhere. After I struck the brother, Dad finally stepped in to stop further damage. He took both boys home and told their father, "If your boys ever lay another hand on my son, I'll be back." That was Dad—a wire-thin, six-foot frame with more fight in it than anyone I'd ever met.

But Dad was in Vietnam now, so I had reverted to my mother's preferred approach of endurance. That tension lived in me every day: endure and suffer now, or fight and suffer later.

Three months into the school year, my mother's patience finally broke. A rock found my face, hitting my mouth with enough force to split my lip and drive my teeth backward. I don't remember falling; I only remember the blood and the hands pulling me upright.

At the hospital, they stitched me from lip to chin, wired my gums, and reset four teeth. For days, I ate through a straw, then graduated to soft food, and finally to anything that didn't require chewing. When the stitches came out, the pain faded, but the targeting didn't.

The assaults resumed almost immediately. My mother went to the school and received the same response every time: reassurance, concern, and empty promises. Finally, she gave me permission to fight back. It felt like oxygen.

During recess one afternoon, the teachers organized a game of flag football. There was no supervision beyond the field, no crowd, and no allies. I chose my moment. I found the boy who had thrown the rock. Without his friends nearby and without warning, I lowered my shoulder and drove into his chest with everything I had—all one hundred and thirty pounds of me. He went down hard, his head hitting the ground with a sound I can still hear. For a split second, I thought I'd killed him, and I realized I didn't feel much remorse.

Teachers rushed in and pulled me away. The boy lay still long enough for fear to catch up to me, and the next thing I knew, I was sitting in the principal's office.

My mother arrived with my three-year-old sister in tow; her anger aimed entirely at the administration. She made me lift my shirt to show the bruises on my ribs and spoke calmly, precisely, about the daily assaults and the school's inaction. I assumed I'd be suspended, but nothing happened. No charges, no punishment, no real consequences for anyone.

What did change, however, was the atmosphere. The attacks stopped. It wasn't because justice had arrived, but because the rules had shifted; I had demonstrated that I would respond, and that was enough. By the end of sixth grade, I understood something no child should have to learn: safety wasn't guaranteed by adults or fairness. It was negotiated—sometimes violently.

Surprisingly, once the fighting stopped, I found myself tutoring the very classmates who had been assaulting me. One mother even called my mom to ask for help with her son. At first, Mom thought it was another setup, but when the two women met at school, it was clear the other mother was a disciplinarian of the highest order. She instructed my classmate to sit and not move while she and Mom had a private conversation.

It was decided I would tutor him on school grounds after hours, and Mom would drive us both home. We ended up becoming inseparable.

Chapter Eleven

Aunt Ethel told us on an ordinary afternoon. There was no buildup and no ceremony—just a statement delivered the way practical people deliver facts they've already made peace with.

"I'm selling Cedar Inn."

That was it. She was retiring. She didn't give us an explanation, and one was not required; we'd seen for ourselves how she struggled to keep going. It was a physical grind she was no longer willing to endure. The bar still ran on weekends, but even that felt more like habit than livelihood. She was tired, and she wanted out.

To her credit, Aunt Ethel recognized the school year was nearly over and promised to stay open until then. All we had to move were our clothes, a few toys, and the small mountain of books Mom and I had accumulated over the year.

Moving in with my grandparents felt inevitable. Dad would be home from Vietnam in three months, and they wanted us close—close enough that love didn't have to wait three or four years between visits. I wanted that, too. Being around my grandparents wrapped me in a warmth that didn't announce itself; it simply existed.

The solitude of Cedar Inn had worn on me. Standing out front every day, swinging a baseball bat and mimicking the stances of Hank Aaron, Roberto Clemente, and Mickey Mantle had stopped being fun; it was just repetition without reward.

Cedar Inn had never been designed for children, but it had given me something rare: distance. A vantage point. I could sit on the stairs and listen without being seen or ride my bike without passing anyone who knew my name. I could exist quietly.

Drexel Avenue, by contrast, announced itself immediately. Row houses pressed shoulder to shoulder—brick and stoop and narrow windows with no space between lives. There was no buffer; everything was close enough to hear: the arguments, the laughter, the music, and the grief. Overgrown lots choked with weeds sat between buildings like neglected pauses. Dogs occupied nearly every backyard, including ours—not as pets, but as vigilant, territorial alarms. Their barking stitched the neighborhood together into a constant, low-level warning. I never set foot in that backyard for fear our dog, Sugar, would rip me to shreds.

There were no white faces. None. Not on the sidewalk, not at the corner, and not passing through. By the time we moved in, the north side of Atlantic City was entirely Black. I didn't think of it in historical terms then—it was simply what I saw. Black faces on every porch, Black kids in the street, and Black churches anchoring the blocks like landmarks you navigated by instinct.

Mom didn't talk about how the neighborhood had come to be that way, and my grandparents, Helen and Harry, had lived there long enough to have watched the area change. But by the time I arrived, whatever transition had happened felt settled—almost invisible. Mom had spent part of her childhood in that house; to her, nothing about it felt imposed or temporary. It just felt like where we were.

At Cedar Inn, Black life had arrived in fragments—men after work, tired voices, and stories carried in late-night conversations. It came filtered through the adult world. Drexel Avenue was total immersion. People knew who I was within days: whose grandson I was, who my mother belonged to, and where my father was stationed. There was no anonymity.

My grandparents' house became a hub. Family passed through constantly, food appeared without planning, and the radio never slept. But the move came with a new set of rules, and one in particular changed everything: I was not allowed to leave the front porch without an escort. Ever.

My grandmother and mother made that clear on the first day. There was no negotiation. This wasn't Maine or Madrid, where I could disappear for hours. They understood this place far better than I did, and they knew I wasn't equipped to navigate it alone.

The house sat just eight blocks from the Boardwalk, but between us and that stretch of lights lay a diffcrent reality. On walks with family, I saw it up close: drug houses operating in plain sight, drunks spilling out of bars at noon, and arguments that turned violent without warning. Armed robberies were discussed the way people talked about the weather. To my family, this wasn't shocking; it was familiar. Known. To me, it felt like the world had suddenly folded inward.

And then there was church. Unlike nearly everything else in my life, St. James AME was not optional. At Loring, Catholic services had been orderly and measured; at St. James, worship was physical.

My grandmother was the secretary of the church and the leader of the choir—roles she held for decades. The church wasn't just where she went on Sundays; it was where she belonged. It had been the family church for generations. For me, attendance wasn't a question. My grandparents bought me a suit reserved for Sundays and Sundays only. It hung in the closet like a uniform—pressed, intentional, and reserved for something that mattered.

St. James was my first full immersion into the Black community as a lived experience. This wasn't the guarded politeness of military life. This was something warmer. Fuller. People greeted one another like they'd survived something together—which, I would later understand, they had. The sermons were delivered with a cadence that made the message unmistakable; the rhythm mattered as much as the words. I felt it before I understood it: this was Black America as sanctuary.

The summer months drifted by slowly. The highlight of my day was our nightly gathering on the front porch after dinner, watching the theater of Drexel Avenue unfold. Loud music spilled from open windows, and kids jumped rope in the street. My grandmother, a great cook and an even better napper, was always the first to drift off as the sun slipped below the rooftops. Her head would sway until her neck snapped upright again, as if startled awake by her own dreams.

The boredom of Drexel Avenue eventually made me feel caged, and one afternoon, I broke Rule Number One. I wanted Dunkin' Donuts. I walked several blocks to Atlantic Avenue, bought them, and came home convinced I'd gone unnoticed. I hadn't. The punishment was swift: I was grounded from all family activities for two weeks—except church. The donuts were distributed to everyone in the house except me.

My grandfather recognized my restlessness and decided to offer an olive branch. As the foreman of the Boardwalk, he often arrived at work at four in the morning, long before the shops opened. This was the "BC" era—Before Casinos—when the place belonged to workers and the sea itself. One evening, he slipped into my bedroom.

"How would you like to go to work with me in the morning?"

Grandpop was soft-spoken, and I studied his face, searching for a clue. Then I saw it—recognition, not judgment. I nodded without speaking, and the tears surprised me. They weren't from fear; they were relief. He reached over, set my alarm for 3:00 a.m., and walked out.

My grandfather never did anything without consulting my grandmother, so I knew this had been approved. That alone made it feel official. Safe.

The next morning, in the darkness of a mid-July dawn, it was just the two of us walking and munching on donuts. My grandparents never owned a car; everything happened on foot. I knew Grandpop was a World War II veteran, though he rarely spoke of it. That morning, he said just enough.

"Your father is a strong man," he told me. "But when he gets back, don't ask him about his experience. Give him space. Besides—he just missed a year of your life. It's going to take him a while."

The words landed somewhere between comfort and confusion. Before I could ask anything, we reached his office, and the conversation ended there. I was grateful for that.

Chapter Twelve

What Grandpop offered me that night wasn't work—it was permission.

By the time most people stirred, we were already on the Boardwalk. The air smelled faintly of salt and yesterday's rain. Most mornings, we didn't say much—we didn't need to. We fell into a daily rhythm and a pace that required no talk. In those early hours, no one watched or corrected me. I wasn't being measured; I was simply there, moving forward while the rest of the city lagged behind.

On that first day, Grandpop pressed five dollars into my palm and gave me a return time and three rules: be back by one, stay on the Boardwalk, and do not cross into Ventnor City, the town just to the south.

Not much was open at 5:30 a.m., but one bike rental shop cracked its doors just long enough to hand me a set of wheels—often for free, and always without question. It took a few mornings to understand why. The owner squinted at me once, trying to make sense of a kid alone at dawn, and then his face cleared. "You must be Harry's grandson." A smile as wide as the Grand Canyon spread across my face. He never charged me again. The bike wasn't just transportation; it was movement handed over without paperwork.

I rode north toward the lighthouse where a narrow inlet met the open Atlantic. Fishing boats idled out in a quiet procession, their engines low and patient. Seagulls and terns wheeled overhead, crying out as they tracked the boats, dipping close enough to skim the water before rising again, hopeful and precise. No one spoke; the ocean did enough talking for all of us.

By seven, I'd crossed nearly the entire length of the Boardwalk—four miles end to end—doubling back as the city slowly stretched awake. On the return trip, donut and pastry shops waved me in. "On the house," they'd say. I was Harry's grandson. White shop owners, Black shop owners—all of them smiled the same way.

By the time I reached Steel Pier, workers were unlocking gates and sweeping yesterday out of the way. I made myself useful, hauling supplies and running errands, earning companionship, food, and the occasional free ride. No one questioned why a twelve-year-old was there alone; I belonged by association.

By 10:00 a.m., the beach began to fill. Umbrellas bloomed like flowers and the noise arrived in layers. Somewhere that summer, I started paying close attention to the women on the beach. My body began reacting to the world in ways my mind couldn't explain—an awareness I didn't have words for and didn't yet want to examine too closely.

When the Boardwalk became too crowded to ride at noon, I'd return the bike and drift between shops, waiting for the heat to crest before walking home. When I handed Grandpop what remained of the five dollars, he assumed I hadn't enjoyed myself, but he was wrong. Those mornings were mine. No fear, no supervision—just space. I watched how the city breathed and how kindness passed quietly between strangers. Seeing Black and white families sharing the same stretch of sand made me feel something close to relief. This was how things were supposed to look.

The letter arrived the morning after Grandpop and I began our walks. Mom tore it open at the kitchen table and read it once—fast, focused—then handed me a single page.

"I have to report to Tyndall Air Force Base on August 30."

That was it. No buildup. Just the next set of orders folded neatly in an envelope. Later that evening, I finally asked, "Where is Tyndall Air Force Base?" No one knew.

Geography came to me through baseball. Newspapers were my textbooks—AP New York, UPI Boston. Cities lived first in bylines, then on maps. I knew all fifty states and their capitals because of box scores, not classrooms, but Tyndall hadn't crossed my radar. Grandpop went into the front room and returned with an atlas. He flipped to Florida, slid it toward me without a word, and left.

Mom and I searched the pages, growing frustrated. The legend didn't mention the base. We found Panama City, but Florida was too big, too awkwardly shaped; nothing lined up. Grandpop returned, saw our angst, flipped the page, and pointed. He'd already looked it up.

The panhandle. "There," he said. Tyndall sat just outside Panama City, right on the Gulf of Mexico. Mom and I smiled at each other. Warm weather. Beaches without winter coats. Atlantic City had sand, but it also had the cold. Florida sounded like mercy.

I called Kim that night. We'd stayed in touch by phone, pretending distance could be negotiated if you tried hard enough. When I told her about the move, her silence said everything. Her family wasn't military; none of this was normal to her. It stung more than I expected. Like kids always do, we promised to stay in touch, but we both knew how this worked. Military moves didn't end relationships loudly; they dissolved them quietly.

What I didn't understand then was why neither of my parents paused over one detail: we were moving south. It was a region that had dominated the news for years because of civil rights resistance and reckoning. Perhaps they assumed geography couldn't change us, or maybe it felt easier not to connect the dots until they were unavoidable. Either way, the letter had done its job. My time with my grandparents now had an expiration date. Military life—patient, methodical, and relentless—had reclaimed me.

Dad came home in early August. From a distance, he looked the same—same posture, same walk. But as he got closer, I could see a shift in his face. It wasn't damage, exactly, but a weight, as if something invisible had settled into him and decided to stay. He hugged Mom first, long and tight, as if he needed to anchor himself before letting go. Then he hugged us kids, one by one, before turning to Granny and Grandpop with stories and smiles that felt practiced.

He was exhausted. The adrenaline of the return carried him for a few hours, then disappeared. For two days, I barely saw him. Even Mom gave him space. Months of constant alertness collapsed into heavy, uninterrupted sleep. My little sister didn't understand. When she screamed after being told to be quiet, Dad snapped. The spanking that followed was swifter and harder than anything I'd ever seen from him. I froze, trying to reconcile the man who left with the one who had returned.

Was this what war did to people?

I stayed out of his orbit after that. Even once his sleep settled, I kept my distance. I think he noticed. One afternoon, he caught me off guard, looping an arm around my neck and giving me a playful punch to the gut. He smiled and called me "big daddy," a nickname that would last for the rest of his life. That was the man I knew.

I'd grown seven inches while he was gone. We were both six feet tall now. I saw it register on his face—a reminder of time he couldn't reclaim.

After a week of rest, Dad began preparing for the move. But before Florida, he insisted on one stop: Philadelphia, to see Aunt Doris. West Philadelphia looked like a war zone. The plight of the inner city was exacerbated tenfold compared to Atlantic City. It was so dangerous we were told not to even sit on the front porch. Dad was so nervous about the car being stolen that he woke up every few hours to check the window, flipping the porch light on as a deterrent.

We were only in town for twenty-four hours—long enough to hear gunshots and a constant drone of police sirens and barking dogs. That trip shattered any remaining notion that Black Atlantic City was an outlier. Things were about to get worse.

ACT II
LEARNING THE HARD WAY

Chapter Thirteen

August 1970

The air was thick and unmoving, the kind that presses against your chest until breathing feels like a chore. Flags hung limp above the Boardwalk, and the car—tightly packed and lacking air-conditioning—felt like an oven.

We left that morning carrying more luggage than sense, along with stereo equipment Dad had shipped home from overseas. I was sad to leave my grandparents, but the idea of a new place—something entirely unfamiliar—pulled me forward. Dad steered us toward Interstate 95, headed for Baltimore, his birthplace, to visit his mother—a woman none of us truly knew.

We arrived in the early afternoon. Grandma Jean greeted us in a bright floral dress, her light chocolate skin and flowing salt-and-pepper hair catching the sun. She cried when she saw Dad, and while her joy was real, something unsettled lingered behind it—a hesitation she never quite named. Dad had built a life entirely without her, and standing there, she seemed unsure how to place herself inside it.

She had married years after his birth to a man who treated us politely but distantly, his civility feeling strained. Dad had two half-brothers there; one was close to my age, and we found common ground almost immediately through music. We spent hours in his room playing the same Temptations album over and over, specifically "Ball of Confusion." We didn't talk much—we didn't need to. The music did the work, filling the space where words might have failed.

The other brother was older and had just returned from Vietnam. He stayed mostly apart, distant and cold, moving through the house like someone who didn't intend to stay. He drank constantly and smoked marijuana until the room filled thick enough that I was forced to leave. Once, a man came by and handed him something quietly, without a word. If Dad noticed what his brother was doing—or what he was carrying—he didn't let on. They hadn't grown up together, and whatever connection might have existed felt incomplete, interrupted long before the war entered the picture.

I noticed the contrast anyway. My father had been to Vietnam and had come home intact, at least on the surface. His brother had been drafted and returned changed in ways I couldn't name but couldn't miss. The difference registered deeply, settling somewhere in my mind I wasn't yet ready to examine.

Their home sat in West Baltimore, and on the drive in, I watched the city change. The houses grew closer together, and burn marks still scarred the buildings—remnants of the unrest that followed Dr. King's assassination two years earlier. Some windows were still boarded up, soot climbing the brick like a shadow that refused to fade. I wondered, quietly, if this was a version of America I hadn't been meant to see. And if it was, what that meant for me.

That afternoon, Dad went to see his hero—my great-grandfather, Grandpa Lee. It was the first and only time we met. He was tall and narrow with fair skin and features that mirrored Dad's so clearly there was no question of their bond. His presence was gentle and grounding; watching them together felt like witnessing something being restored.

Years earlier, Dad and Grandpa Lee had slipped unnoticed into places they weren't meant to enter, able to "pass" in a city built on separation. It was a quiet survival skill, learned early. As the sun dropped low, Grandpa Lee called me over. He removed the sunglasses he'd worn all afternoon and placed them carefully in my hands.

"Take care of them," he said. Then he cried. The little boy he had once insisted be allowed to join the living now had a son of his own to pass something on to. I wore those glasses all the way south; after that, I put them away and never touched them again. They felt like something entrusted, not owned. Two years later, Grandpa Lee was gone, and Dad never fully recovered.

When Grandma Jean became pregnant at fifteen, it was Grandpa Lee who had insisted she carry the child to term. He arranged for Dad to be adopted by family—offering protection, stability, and distance. Dad grew up between households and between explanations.

The mystery of his biology persisted during the visit but now was not the time or place to press. That secret would continue to haunt him; a quiet absence that never stopped echoing, leaving room for a thousand guesses—White, Black, or something else entirely. Given our lineage, any of those answers were possible, but Dad has learned early that the world's need to label him was their burden, not his.

They tried to categorize him constantly, and they failed just as often. When he checked "Black" on government forms, officials would question it, seek to correct it, or openly doubt it. It angered him—not because he was unsure, but because they were. Dad carried the unknowable parts of his history without apology; he didn't need a name to know exactly where he stood.

Chapter Fourteen

Dad decided we needed one last history lesson before leaving Baltimore. He drove us downtown, skirting the water where the Inner Harbor had carried ships for centuries—vessels of commerce, war, and human cargo. Dad talked as he always did, stitching the past together as the city blurred past the windows: Fort McHenry, the War of 1812, Francis Scott Key, Babe Ruth, and Frederick Douglass. He knew the names and the dates, but he pointedly avoided the wounds.

At one point, he slowed near a white-owned movie theater he used to sneak into with his grandfather. He laughed at the memory—a hard, loud laugh—as if he'd pulled off a perfect crime and was still savoring the getaway. Then the tour ended. The Bennettmobile turned south.

Interstate 95 cut through Virginia's rolling green hills, smooth pavement slicing through quiet countryside. A warm breeze poured in through the open windows. Dad was the only one in our family who had ever traveled below the Mason-Dixon Line.

Just south of Richmond, we merged onto Interstate 85 toward Charlotte. We drove for hours, well into the night, before Dad finally pulled off near Greensboro. The motel was plain—two beds, no frills, and an outdoor kennel for dogs. I hated motels. Mom and Dad took one bed, my sisters claimed the other, and I slept on the floor, my lower back protesting the entire next morning.

Heidi was the real victim of the night. She wasn't just our dog; she was family. A dachshund, four years old, small-bodied and stubborn, she had a bark far bigger than her frame. Dad had brought her home as a Christmas surprise in 1966 back in Maine, and while she was officially a gift for Karen, she belonged to all of us. Heidi was an indoor dog, fiercely loyal to Karen—Karen's bed was her bed. She had followed us from Maine to Cedar Inn to Drexel Avenue, and now south to Florida.

That night in Greensboro, she was put outside in a kennel, confused and furious. Around ten o'clock, she made her feelings known to anyone within earshot. When the phone in the room rang, Dad didn't argue or explain. He slipped out quietly and returned just as quietly, carrying Heidi against his chest like contraband. She slept beside Karen the rest of the night, finally at peace.

Morning came, and Dad and I walked into the motel restaurant first. The room went silent for a heartbeat. Then, Mom and my sisters entered and sat at our table. Every head turned. Forks hovered midair; conversations died on the spot. What they saw was a white man—at least, that is what they assumed—with a tall Black kid trailing behind him, only to be joined by the rainbow of melanin that made up the rest of our family.

Dad had checked in alone the night before, which wasn't a strategy so much as simple logistics; someone had to stay in the car with us kids. I wondered then if he realized where we were, or if, as a history junkie, he just failed to connect the dots. I certainly hadn't. We sat down anyway. A waitress approached—pleasant, southern, and efficient, with a white apron and a pencil tucked behind her ear.

Behind Dad, eyes bored into us. One woman stared openly, whispered to the man beside her, and then stared even harder. She watched so intently that she missed her mouth with a glass of milk, soaking her blouse. "Damn it," she snapped. Mom and I shook with laughter. Dad turned, confused, then caught on and smirked, muttering a word under his breath he rarely used. It began with a *B*.

Only later would I understand Greensboro's place in the struggle for Civil Rights. What it meant to sit down and refuse to move. At the time, all I knew was the discomfort of another unexplained historical moment my parents chose not to share.

The road carried us through Atlanta without stopping. We flew at sixty-five miles an hour past the only history I was certain of: the Braves and Hank Aaron. To me, that was the entirety of a civil rights education—grace under pressure. Remarkably, Dad the historian remained quiet as we passed through the city.

Outside Montgomery, Dad pulled into a gas station, then immediately pulled right back out just as I was opening the car door. "Get your ass back in the car," he barked. Whatever he spotted that spooked him, I still don't know. A few miles later, on a deserted stretch of highway, I relieved myself in the bushes, the dog and I hiding together in the weeds.

Within twenty-four hours, we had passed Richmond, Greensboro, and Atlanta, skirted Birmingham, and came close to Selma—names that meant nothing to me then. What I did know was that the country felt foreign. It was worse than Spain; the language was wrong, the rhythm was wrong, and the air carried a tension I couldn't name. Southerners spoke a version of English that sounded unfinished, with stretched words and disappearing letters. Dad hated it. "Y'all." "Ain't."

The farther south we traveled, the more the land flattened. Red clay gave way to sand and pine forests. Towns appeared half-forgotten—rusted cars, sagging trailers, clothes worn thin by heat and time. Then I saw them: two signs discarded on the side of the road.

BLACK ENTRANCE. WHITE ENTRANCE.

They looked new—too clean, as if they'd been taken down recently but not yet erased. They stayed with me for the next ninety miles. *Is this how we would live?* A violent southern downpour answered that question briefly, erasing the road and swallowing all visibility before vanishing as quickly as it had arrived. Steam rose from the asphalt and the sunlight became blinding. It felt unreal, like a warning.

Panama City finally came into view as we rolled south on U.S. Highway 231. There was no bridge announcing our arrival, just road, heat, and a town that looked nothing like the Florida I had pictured. Dad turned left onto U.S. Highway 98, heading east. We drove nearly ten miles before water appeared on both sides. We crossed the Dupont Bridge, and on the far side sat Tyndall Air Force Base. There was no traditional gate—just signs, warnings, and rules.

To the north were the houses, one of which would become ours. To the south sat a single structure: Tyndall Elementary School, where my sisters would start in two weeks. Dad stopped at the police station for directions to our temporary housing, and after twelve hours in the backseat, the blood returned to my legs like a gift.

That night, the television glowed as I tried to learn the area through the local news. The accents were still a strange, impenetrable sound to my ears; I caught myself taking a beat just to understand the anchors. Then, I saw something called the "Tyndall Report"—delivered by a Second Lieutenant who was definitely not southern. It was a welcomed relief. I would eventually learn that Tyndall Air Force Base wasn't just our new home; it was the area's largest employer. The military bubble had closed around us once again.

Chapter Fifteen

Dad was up early the next morning, already in uniform and moving as if the day had been waiting for him. He headed to the hospital where he would be working as an administrator and returned around eleven with a sergeant he introduced as our sponsor—the man assigned to help us get settled.

The first problem was housing. Dad was on the list for base quarters, but the house intended for us was still occupied by another military family. We had a three-month wait ahead of us. Our sponsor drove us off-base to a place called Treasure Cove Cottages, located just outside Tyndall on Highway 98. The property sat back in a thin stand of trees draped in Spanish moss, close enough to the road that the sound of traffic never truly disappeared.

The landlord was a genial white woman who made her living renting to military families. She greeted us without hesitation, seemingly unfazed by the fact that our family didn't fit into the neat categories people usually preferred. We toured a two-bedroom, one-bath cottage and signed the papers on the spot.

There were about fifteen detached cottages arranged around a shared, U-shaped gravel drive. The ground was mostly sand and scrub, though toward the back of the property, the landlord's own home overlooked East Bay, offering spectacular views of the sunset.

Inside our cottage, however, the view was less impressive. It felt as though it had been furnished with whatever was cheapest and closest at hand. The linoleum floor had buckled and peeled where rot had eaten the wood underneath, and the carpet was a dingy, threadbare yellow shag, flattened by years of footsteps. Everything smelled faintly musty, as if the walls had absorbed too many humid summers and had never quite exhaled.

The sofa bed in the living room was mine for the next three months. Its mattress was so thin it felt like the springs were taking an inventory of my body, leaving impressions in my back and legs every night. The floor might have been an improvement—if not for that yellow carpet, which looked like it had hosted its own entire ecosystem.

Once we had a roof over our heads, the next order of business was school. I waited until later in the afternoon when our sponsor finally gave us the name: Rosenwald Junior High. He said it casually, as if it were a mere formality, and then he told us where it was.

Rosenwald sat in what was then the poorest section of Panama City, right in the heart of the Black community. The bus ride would take thirty to forty minutes, depending on traffic. All of us from Tyndall—military kids—were being sent there, although another junior high sat much closer to the base.

At first, we were told the move was to relieve overcrowding, but that explanation didn't last long. It wasn't about convenience; it was about desegregation. This was part of the court-mandated busing program being implemented nationwide. In Florida, this was the very first year of the effort—nearly a decade after similar movements had ignited protests elsewhere, most of them led by white parents.

Military families were treated differently. We were considered transient—accustomed to change and practiced in difference. We went where we were told and were expected to make it work. In places without military kids to absorb the colonial shock of the experiment, the system often fractured quickly. Outwardly, it looked like a bad idea. Inwardly, we kids never talked about it. We just got on the bus.

Chapter Sixteen

The next day, we drove into Panama City to register me. No one explained much on the way; the decision had already been made.

The neighborhood announced itself before the school did. Across the street sat a row of houses raised on cinder blocks, their wood slats warped so badly you could see straight into the rooms through the gaps. Some leaned left, as if exhausted; others leaned right, as if they'd simply stopped trying to stay upright. Around the corner, another cluster of homes appeared brighter—Caribbean colors, sun-faded and peeling, yet still worn down to the bones. It wasn't the kind of poverty I knew how to name. It wasn't a statistic. It was texture. It was air. It was the way a place told you, without speaking, what it had been denied.

To the right of the school, behind a chain-link fence, sat an oval dirt track—scuffed and packed down, with stubborn patches of green forcing their way through cracks in the earth. Inside the oval, trampled grass and knee-high weeds gave the center a wild, neglected look. The school itself—a red brick exterior with a sign that read Rosenwald Junior High School—looked almost sturdy by comparison. Not proud. Not new. Just standing.

Inside, the front office sat immediately off the entrance, positioned like a sentry post to monitor exactly who came in and who left. The air inside was trapped and stale, humming with the electric buzz of a window unit that struggled against the Florida humidity.

We were led into the office of the school counselor, a man named Mr. Thompson. He sat behind a desk piled with folders, but the one he held in his hands was mine. He spent a long time looking at my transcripts from New Jersey—longer than I expected. My parents sat rigid in their chairs. For Mom, "busing" wasn't just a logistical term; it was a threat, a word that conjured images of uncertainty and vulnerability for her son.

Mr. Thompson finally looked up, his eyes moving from the paper to me. "You've got some impressive marks here, son," he said, a genuine note of respect in his voice. He turned to my father. "Based on these grades, we aren't just going to slot him into the standard curriculum. We are going to put him into our most challenging classes."

Dad didn't offer a smile in return. He wasn't looking for flattery; he was looking for security. He leaned forward, his voice dropping into that low, tactical register he used when he was assessing a mission. He began to interrogate Mr. Thompson about the busing situation—how it worked, who was on those buses, and what happened the moment I stepped off them.

"You have to understand," Mr. Thompson explained, leaning in as if to settle Dad's nerves, "we've been preparing for this. The faculty hasn't just been thrown together. Our teachers were integrated two years ago. We've been working together, Black and white instructors side-by-side, even while Rosenwald was still an all-Black school. We've smoothed out those edges so we can focus on the students."

As he spoke, the door opened and a man with an unmistakable air of authority entered. This was Mr. Spivey, the principal. He didn't just peak in; he walked over and introduced himself with a firm handshake. I couldn't tell if it was happenstance—a principal doing his rounds—or if he truly wanted to size up the new student who had just landed on his doorstep. Either way, his presence added a layer of gravity to the room.

The administrators were polite. Careful. They spoke to my mother in measured tones, as if trying to physically wrap her in the assurance that I would be fine. That I would be safe. That I would be looked after. Mom listened; her purse clutched tightly in her lap. She didn't look convinced.

I didn't know what I was supposed to feel. Rosenwald felt like a place with a history I hadn't earned yet—something heavy beneath the surface, a complicated machine that Mr. Thompson and Mr. Spicer were trying to convince us was ready for me.

Only later would I learn that more than five thousand Rosenwald schools had been built across the South during segregation—institutions created specifically to educate Black children when public systems refused to. They were named after Julius Rosenwald, a Jewish-American clothier and president of Sears, Roebuck and Company. Beginning around 1913, he helped finance schools in places where education for Black students was considered optional, expendable, or even dangerous.

At the end of the day, Dad and Mom signed the forms, picked up my schedule, and nodded at the instructions. Then, we walked back out into the thick Florida heat. As we walked back to the car, Mom expressed her displeasure without uttering a single curse word. Dad remained quiet, searching for a way to solve the "Rosenwald problem." But the only solution was to live off-base, and that was a non-starter. Free military housing versus rent or a mortgage—the math was easy. Rosenwald it was.

Dad reached for the door handle just as a loud, sharp pop echoed from the street. Before the sound had even faded, he had dropped instinctively bracing against the car for cover. It was only a distant car backfiring, but in that split second, the sound hadn't been a mechanical failure; it had been a threat. Mom and I stood frozen; watching him, entirely unaware that we just saw the first real tell of a war he had brought home with him—a shadow that would eventually grow to define the years to come.

Chapter Seventeen

The bus ride took about forty minutes. That was the number everyone used, but it wasn't precise. Some mornings it felt shorter, like the road was helping us along; other mornings it stretched, every stoplight an obstacle, every turn another reminder of how far away Rosenwald really was.

Wilson drove.

He was Black, probably in his early fifties, with wavy hair slicked back neatly and a smile that never seemed forced. He greeted every kid the same way: "Good morning, my friend," whether they answered him or not. If he saw you outside school, on the street, or at the base, the greeting didn't change. Everybody was his friend, even if they didn't know how to return the favor.

Since we were still in temporary housing, Dad dropped me at the motor pool each morning to catch the bus. I liked arriving early. Wilson would already be there, leaning against the bus or sitting inside with the other drivers, joking and talking before the day had decided what it was going to be.

The drivers were all older than my parents, men who had grown up in the Jim Crow South. It was a world I couldn't fully comprehend, but I sensed it in the way they spoke to one another—measured, familiar, and layered with a history I hadn't yet been given. Black and white drivers stood together, sharing cigarettes and coffee. On the surface, at least, they moved like men who trusted each other. I loved being there. For a few minutes each morning, I wasn't a student or a social problem to be solved. I was just one of the boys.

I always took the seat right behind Wilson so we could talk—about nothing important, and about everything. He didn't pry and he didn't warn me; he just drove, steady and sure, as if the road belonged to him.

The bus filled in stages. White, Black, and every shade between boarded in no particular order, mixed together the way military kids always were—loud, familiar, and unguarded. There were no invisible lines being honored, no ritualized distance. Most of us had grown up in integrated schools on or near bases, places where Jim Crow existed only in history books, if he existed at all.

Outside the windows, Panama City slid past, the neighborhoods changing gradually, and then all at once. Houses thinned and streets narrowed. The air felt heavier the closer we got.

No one talked much as Rosenwald came into view that first day. This was a new experience for everyone on board. Local students were already gathered—Black students, mostly—standing in small clusters, watching the fleet of buses approach. Six large, blue Air Force buses rolled in that morning. Mine was the second. I stayed seated as long as I could, letting the other kids move past me. My hands were damp; my mouth was dry. If my bladder had anything left in it, I would've lost control right there.

The memory of sixth grade hovered close—close enough to touch. I told myself that whatever had happened before couldn't possibly prepare me for what was coming now. The thought didn't help. I sat frozen, staring straight ahead, as the bus continued to empty.

Wilson glanced back at me. "You good, my friend?"

I nodded. I wasn't.

I stood slowly, every movement deliberate, as if sudden motion might shatter something fragile inside me. The aisle felt longer than it had any right to be. My shirt clung to my back, soaked through with a sweat that had nothing to do with the

Florida heat. At the door, I paused. I looked back once, catching Wilson's eye. He smiled—wide, warm, and reassuring. It helped. Not much, but enough.

I stepped down.

Before my foot even hit the pavement, I felt them: eyes. They watched me openly. Not hostile, not welcoming—just present. Curious. Measuring. They were trying to decide where I fit, or if I fit at all. I kept my head down, eyes locked on the gravel, afraid that if I stopped moving, I'd stop entirely. Each step felt like a massive effort; each breath felt borrowed.

I made it across the lot and into the building without incident. No one said a word. No one had to. Behind me, I heard the bus doors hiss shut. The engine growled as Wilson pulled away, taking whatever protection the ride had offered along with him.

Chapter Eighteen

Homeroom sat at the far end of the school. The hallway filled quickly with seventh, eighth, and ninth graders who, on the first day of school, didn't just walk straight to class. They catch up with old friends, talk far too much, and fill the corridors with noise loud enough to drown out a 747. It felt less like the start of school and more like a reunion—voices overlapping, laughter echoing, bodies stopping short in doorways to reconnect.

Even then, the lines were forming.

The Black kids from the surrounding neighborhood stayed close to one another, watching, measuring their new white counterparts. Many of them had known each other their entire lives. The white kids—almost all from Tyndall—clustered by where they lived on base, not by race. Kids from the same housing areas moved together, loud and familiar, already sorted by geography and routine. I found my locker and moved on.

Inside the classroom, old desks were arranged in neat rows, all facing forward. I took a seat in the back, choosing distance over visibility. Slumping low, I tried to disappear into the furniture. If someone wanted to see me, they'd have to turn around. Most didn't.

The room filled. Voices rose and settled. Chairs scraped the floor, and a low hum of anticipation hung in the air. Then Ms. Jones entered.

She was a Black woman, poised and deliberate, dressed simply but sharply—the kind of teacher who didn't need volume to command a room. She didn't rush. She didn't smile. She took her place at the front of the class like someone who had been standing there long before we arrived. She surveyed the room once—slow and deliberate—her eyes lingering just long enough on faces that already knew her before moving on. A few of the local Black students straightened instinctively.

"Good morning," she said. The response came back uneven. She didn't look up.

"I said GOOD MORNING."

This time, the class answered together. She nodded once, then started roll call. She read two names then stopped.

"Young man in the back," she said, without looking up. "Sit up straight."

The command snapped through the room. I obeyed immediately, unfolding my long frame, shoulders back, eyes forward. I assumed that would be the end of it. It wasn't. She looked directly at me. "Where are you from?"

The question landed like a thrown object. I opened my mouth. Nothing came out.

"How many places have you lived?"

Still nothing.

"What does your father do?"

My throat tightened. The room shrank. Every eye was on me now—especially the ones that had never seen a new face stay under a teacher's gaze this long.

"What are your interests outside of school?"

"How are your grades?"

The questions came fast—precise, relentless. This wasn't curiosity, it was an interrogation. I tried to answer. My lips moved and sound followed, but it came out wrong—thin, shaky, and barely recognizable as speech.

"Come on, Mr. Bennett. We don't have all day."

My tongue felt thick. My mouth dry. The silence stretched long enough to hurt. Then something shifted. Ms. Jones' expression softened—just slightly. She tilted her head, the smallest adjustment, and then—so quickly I might've imagined it—she winked. Only at me.

The room didn't notice. They were still watching, still waiting. But that wink landed like a lifeline. I swallowed, cleared my throat, and tried again. This time, the words came. Slow at first, then steadier, I answered every question: where I'd lived, what my father did, and how I performed in school.

As I spoke, the room changed. The tension eased, replaced by interest. A few of the local kids turned fully in their seats now, no longer pretending not to look. Ms. Jones listened closely—too closely. She leaned into my answers, pulling details out and pressing just enough to keep me standing without knocking me over.

Some students smiled. A few whispered. One voice near the front cut through the room: "Are you American?"

I still carried a semblance of that quirky New England accent from my days in Maine. A ripple of laughter followed—not cruel, just uncertain. Ms. Jones didn't scold, but she didn't laugh, either

"Alright now, Ms. Smarty Pants," she said evenly, eyes still on her attendance book. "Mr. Bennett has an answer for you. It says here you lived outside the United States." She looked up at me.

"Yes, ma'am," I said. I wasn't in the habit of "yes ma'am-ing" anybody. My mother didn't require it. But here, in this room, it felt right. I explained that I'd gone to kindergarten through second grade in Madrid.

Another student asked, "Where's Madrid?"

As if anticipating the question, Ms. Jones turned to the world map mounted on the wall. She picked up the long wooden pointer and, without hesitation, tapped Spain. A few heads tilted upward; others leaned forward. Not bad for a pre-algebra teacher.

She spoke with the cadence of the South—drawn-out syllables and soft edges—but there was nothing soft about her mind. She knew exactly what she was doing. By the time roll call ended, I wasn't invisible anymore. I hadn't meant to be seen. But I had been. And the day had only just begun.

Chapter Nineteen

The gym sat apart from the rest of the school, its wide doors propped open in a losing battle against the heat. Early September in Florida didn't announce itself; it pressed down. For a kid from the Northeast, it was suffocating. Just walking across the floor pulled sweat to the surface and standing still didn't help—the air clung to you like wet fabric.

We gathered on a section of bleachers pulled out from the wall, sneakers scraping metal as we climbed into place. The gym felt like a contradiction. While much of Rosenwald showed its wear, this room had been protected. The hardwood floor was pristine, polished to a dull shine, especially for a school that bore so many signs of neglect elsewhere. At center court, our mascot stared back at us: a snarling bulldog, teeth bared, frozen mid-growl. Maroon and white lines cut clean paths across the floor, the colors repeated along the walls and railings. Someone had decided long ago that this space mattered.

For most boys, physical education was the class you circled on your schedule. For me, it had always been something to endure—not because I wasn't athletic, though I didn't know that yet, but because I simply didn't come from a family of athletes. No one pushed me toward sports or framed them as important. Baseball and bowling were the only things I'd ever done, and even those felt incidental.

That changed in a nanosecond when Coach walked in. Everyone just called him Coach. No last name; no need for one. He was a Black man in his early thirties with a gruff voice and an easy smile, dressed in African safari shorts and a wide-brimmed safari hat. That hat would become inseparable from him—so much so that years later, I couldn't picture Coach without it. He took roll like no one I'd ever seen. Some names he hollered, stretching syllables and landing emphasis in all the wrong places on purpose; others he announced like a radio play-by-play, complete with commentary. When he got to mine, he didn't hesitate.

"Benneeeeeett."

The name echoed off the cinderblock walls, coming back heavier than it left. In the ten years I would know him, I don't think he ever once called me by my first name. Coach had that balance adults spend a lifetime chasing: discipline and warmth, authority and humor. You could tell immediately he loved his job. More than that, he loved shaping boys into something sturdier than they were when they arrived.

We were assigned lockers and told to change that first week. Like most pre-teen boys, the idea of stripping down to your underwear while others pretended not to look was uncomfortable at best. Most of us avoided it by wearing gym shorts under our street clothes—an unspoken agreement, universally honored.

I arrived early one day during week two and caught Coach joking with a group of white students. They were loose, laughing hard. When the Black students arrived, the energy shifted. I overheard one kid mutter something about Coach talking to "whitey." I wondered what he was supposed to do—ignore half the class? I muttered "idiots" under my breath, a little louder than I should have. No one heard.

After roll call, Coach sent us outside to the track for four laps—one mile. Up close, the oval looked different than it had on registration day. It was still dirt and uneven, but it had been trimmed back, the weeds pulled, the path more defined. Someone had tried. That effort mattered.

The heat wrapped tighter outside. Sweat ran freely now, soaking shirts within minutes. I ran hard anyway, letting the movement burn off the tension that had nowhere else to go.

Another kid kept pace with me—Black, shorter by a few inches, and already built like an adult. We finished nearly two minutes ahead of everyone else. Coach waved us over and handed us water in tiny cone-shaped paper cups he already had prepared. I tried a little small talk, desperate for anyone besides a teacher to speak with me, but it went nowhere.

Back on the field, Coach split us into teams for flag football. He mixed us deliberately—Black and white together—so evenly it couldn't be mistaken for chance. The kickoff skipped end-over-end across the dirt, and the returner's flag was pulled almost immediately.

Coach crouched and drew a play in the dirt with his finger. We leaned in as he explained it twice, yet still, no one made eye contact.

When we lined up, a realization hit us all at once: blocking meant touching. The ball was snapped. No one blocked. The pass intended for me hit the ground. The coaches lit into us—not for fear or hesitation, but for a lack of effort. They never once named the thing sitting between us; they didn't have to.

As the period wore on, something shifted. The second play was better; the third, better still. Sweat blurred the lines. Fear loosened, words were exchanged, and hands finally met shoulders. Trust crept in where silence had been. For that hour, teamwork won. When class ended, Coach clapped me on the shoulder in front of everyone, praising my "outstanding performance." It was ridiculous, and everyone knew it—including me—but it felt like a start.

Back in the locker room, however, the world snapped back into place. Black kids on one side, white kids on the other. And me, somewhere in between, changing quietly by myself. The showers sat unused; no one wanted to be naked in front of anyone else. We all washed up in the sinks instead, a routine that would last for months. Fortunately, this was sixth period, so I could go home and shower in the comfort of my own bathroom.

Coach kept pushing—gently, patiently. He encouraged conversation and paired kids together, letting time do the work he knew force never could. On the field, effort was rewarded. Once the whistle blew, old habits returned.

One afternoon toward the end of my first week, Dad asked how school was going, and for the first time, I didn't know how to answer. Rosenwald was a puzzle—cold, distant, and confusing. Until we moved into our permanent house, the white kids had little reason to know me beyond the bus. I was temporary. The Black students felt the same way. Outside of gym, not one Black student spoke to me that first week—nor for several weeks after that.

Chapter Twenty

While Dad was in Vietnam, I went through a rapid growth spurt—seven inches in twelve months, most of it in the final three. By the time we arrived in Florida, I stood just over six feet tall and weighed a mere 135 pounds, despite eating everything in sight.

My knees had been aching for months, a deep, grinding pain that flared without warning. Some days it felt like someone had taken a hammer to the soft tissue just below my kneecaps. I collapsed more than once doing nothing more than walking.

Eventually, the pain could no longer be ignored. Dad took me to the hospital at Tyndall Air Force Base, the same one where he worked. The building felt familiar to him—corridors he walked daily—but for me, it carried the quiet dread of antiseptic smells and long waits. The orthopedist studied the X-rays longer than I liked. Without much ceremony, my left leg was placed in a cast from hip to ankle. I knew the doctor's diagnosis of a broken leg was wrong—both my knees hurt—but I didn't question authority.

Mom blamed herself for not bringing me in sooner, while Dad said very little. I tried to act tougher than I felt, but the reality of immobility sank in quickly. The cast now dictated everything—how I sat, how I slept, and how I moved through the world. Gym class, my one reliable outlet, was gone for the foreseeable future.

The first weekend after the cast was set, Dad decided we needed a break. It would be our first trip to the beach since arriving in Florida, and nothing in my Atlantic City upbringing had prepared me for what we found. This wasn't a boardwalk town—no arcades, no steel piers, no hotels stacked shoulder to shoulder. As we pulled in, a sign welcomed us to *The World's Most Beautiful Beaches*. They weren't kidding.

The sand was blindingly white—so fine it actually squeaked underfoot—and the Gulf stretched out in calm, rolling layers of blue and green. The waves didn't crash so much as arrive, folding over themselves like a mother pulling a blanket up around a sleeping child. I had never seen sand so bright or water so clear. It was hot, but not oppressive, softened by a light breeze that made breathing feel effortless.

Dad waded into the shallows with my sisters, laughing, splashing, entirely at ease. I couldn't go in because of the cast, so Mom filled plastic beach buckets and carried the Gulf to me instead. She poured the cool salt water over my leg, then used what was left to rub my shoulders and back. Within two hours I had turned several shades darker. My first Florida sunburn would peel for a week.

What struck me most wasn't the water or the heat; it was the people. On our stretch of beach, everyone was white. And unlike at school, or on the bus, there was no hesitation in their presence. When they noticed my cast, strangers approached without pretense—men and women alike—asking what happened and wishing me well like it was the most natural thing in the world.

There was no edge. No weighing of intentions. Just kindness. It caught me off guard, and then it unsettled me. I recognized this version of America. This was the world I grew up in—the one that had felt "normal" before Florida began teaching me rules I hadn't yet mastered. Sitting there with salt drying on my skin, I made a quiet promise not to let Rosenwald rewrite everything I believed about people. I had no idea how hard that would be.

Back at school, the cast changed everything. Wilson made sure I had space on the bus, guarding the bench seat behind him as my personal throne. White students offered help carrying books and holding doors, slowing their pace so I could keep up. Concern replaced indifference almost overnight.

For my Black classmates, the reaction was different. They noticed the cast, but it didn't invite them closer; if anything, it sharpened the distance. A few looked with curiosity, others with something closer to suspicion. The cast didn't make me more familiar to them—it made me more foreign. I was already different; now I was visibly being treated differently by the white students, and that distinction mattered. The attention felt temporary, almost transactional, as if the plaster explained me in a way words never could. I hadn't changed. Only my visibility had.

And in that noticing, something else began to shift—subtly, unevenly, but undeniably. I had no idea what it would cost once the cast finally came off.

Chapter Twenty-One

The saw whirred to life, its vibration buzzing through my leg as the doctor cut away the plaster. Both my parents stood in the room watching—Dad calm and familiar in his workplace, Mom tense, eyes fixed on every movement.

When the cast finally split and fell away, I didn't wait for instructions. Youthful bravado took over. I stood up on my own, eager to prove a point—to them, to myself, to anyone watching.

Big mistake. My leg folded instantly beneath me, atrophied and unprepared, and I went down hard, splayed across the hospital floor before anyone could react. There was a brief stunned silence. Then the doctor burst out laughing. So did Dad.

Mom did not find it funny. She rushed toward me, furious and frightened, scolding both of them as they tried—and failed—to contain their amusement. I lay there, embarrassed and confused, my confidence evaporating faster than the plaster dust on the floor. I didn't find it funny either. Without the cast, there was nothing explaining me. No visible marker inviting patience. No reason for special handling.

The bus ride changed almost immediately. Wilson still greeted me warmly, but the bench seat was no longer my personal throne. My classmates reclaimed their usual spots. Conversations resumed around me, rather than with me. No one was cruel; they simply moved on. At school, teachers stopped asking how I was doing. The brief novelty of concern had expired, and I blended back into the background of movement and noise.

Some of the connections held. A few kids still walked with me between classes, and the names I'd learned didn't vanish overnight. But the effortless attention—the kind that required nothing from me—was gone.

Gym class returned me to motion, though my knees protested with dull, grinding reminders of the growth that had caused this in the first place. Coach didn't say much about the cast coming off. He gave me a single nod, like a checkpoint cleared, and folded me back into the routine. The field didn't care whether I'd been injured; teams mixed the same way, and the sweat leveled us again. Physical contact returned. I moved cautiously at first, then with more confidence as my body remembered what it was capable of.

Black classmates who'd once only noticed me because of the cast now watched how I moved, how I played, and how I carried myself when there was nothing left to excuse a mistake. The white students did the same. There was no cruelty in it, just assessment. I understood something then that I hadn't before: belonging wasn't a gift. It was earned—and re-earned—every single day.

Outside the gym, the lines still existed. Lunch tables told their own quiet stories of segregation, and the hallways funneled people back into familiar, comfortable patterns. Rosenwald didn't transform overnight just because one boy had worn plaster for a month. But something inside me had shifted. I'd learned the hard difference between being noticed and being known.

Chapter Twenty-Two

Three months into seventh grade, little changed. My relationships were sparse. The few classmates who had stayed by my side after my cast was removed were people I never saw after school hours. Honestly, I was lonely. Between the move from New Jersey and the transition to Florida, I was nearly eighteen months into an existence that didn't include a single close friendship with someone my own age.

Then something slipped through the vents of my locker. Rosenwald lockers had narrow slats cut into the metal doors—just wide enough for air, just wide enough for a folded piece of paper. When I opened mine one morning, a note fell to the floor. At first, I assumed it was something official—maybe a summons from the office or a correction from a teacher.

I picked it up. The paper was saturated with perfume—sharp, floral, impossible to ignore. The scent clung to my hands, then my books, then the very air around me. A few students nearby drifted closer, pretending to search their own lockers while surreptitiously taking it in. They didn't need to say anything. The implication was obvious. Someone had been paying attention.

I didn't read it there. I stuffed the note into my pocket and moved on, my face warm and my pulse quickened by a sensation I hadn't felt since arriving in Florida: attention that wasn't accidental. In class, while roll was being called, I opened it just enough to check for a name. There wasn't one.

The letter ran two pages, front and back. It was thoughtful and personal; the words weren't clumsy or rushed. Whoever wrote it had taken her time. She mentioned my intelligence—not as flattery, but as an observation. That detail stayed with me.

You don't call someone smart unless you've really been watching them. The last line was simple: *Can we talk?*

At lunch, I sat where I always sat—alone, slightly removed from the center of the room. I ate slowly, scanning faces without being obvious, wondering if the author was nearby, watching me read between bites. Every glance felt loaded. Every smile felt like it might mean something.

The next day, another note appeared. Then another. They arrived with quiet consistency, always between first and second period. Whoever she was, she knew the rhythm of the building. The notes didn't escalate so much as they deepened—less mystery, more intention. Still, there was no name. No signature.

At night, after my parents went to bed, I reread them. I didn't do it because of what they promised, but because of what they contradicted. I had come to believe I was invisible at Rosenwald—present, but unacknowledged. These notes suggested otherwise. I wasn't yet sure whether that was something I could trust.

Adam and his sister Liz, who was two years our senior, were among the few friends who had stuck by me post-plaster. Adam and I shared several classes. Like me, he was a military kid—new, adaptable, and unburdened by the unspoken rules everyone else seemed to understand. We lived in different housing areas on Tyndall, so school was the only place our paths crossed, but he was my first real friend there—the kind you find when both of you are just trying to survive unfamiliar ground.

He asked why I kept checking my locker like I was expecting mail. I brushed it off, but secrets have a way of leaking. The following Monday, Adam caught her.

He didn't see her face clearly—just the motion of a hand slipping a folded note through the vent before disappearing down the hall. Adam was animated when he told me, energized by the proximity to something he knew mattered. He described her slowly, like he was unwrapping a gift on my behalf: Short. Pretty smile. Confident walk.

Then he added the detail that made it harder to breathe.

"She's a cheerleader," he said. "Ninth grade."

That alone would have been enough to rattle me. Then he paused. "And she's Black."

The hallway noise receded. My first reaction wasn't excitement—it was fear. Not fear of her, but of what it meant. I feared the possibility that this wasn't private, or kind, or sincere. I feared I'd misread everything and was walking straight into a situation designed to make me look foolish.

I stood there holding my books, replaying the notes in my head and weighing their tone against the distance I'd felt for weeks. They hadn't been cruel. They hadn't been mocking. They had been deliberate. I still didn't know what that meant, but I knew one thing with certainty: whatever was happening wasn't imaginary anymore, and it wasn't safe to pretend otherwise.

Chapter Twenty-Three

By the time I saw her name, I already knew who she was—Amanda. She signed the next note neatly, deliberately, as if anonymity had served its purpose and no longer mattered. There was no explanation, no apology for the secrecy—just her name at the bottom, followed by a single line that acknowledged what everyone else could see. *How's your leg doing?*

I folded the note and slipped it into my pocket, aware that the ground had shifted again. Being noticed anonymously was one thing; being acknowledged openly was another. Whatever this was becoming, it was no longer happening in the shadows.

At lunch, I did what I always did. I picked up my tray, moved through the line, and headed toward my usual table—off to the side, away from the heavy traffic, a place that required no explanation. I hadn't taken two steps when a voice came up behind me.

"Need help carrying your tray?"

I still walked with a limp that I guess hadn't gone unnoticed. I turned, and she was even prettier than I expected, composed with the kind of stillness that only comes from deep confidence. I declined the help, but before I could talk myself out of it, I asked if she wanted to sit with me.

We sat across from each other, trays between us, and talked as if time wasn't keeping score. I stuttered; she waited. My food went untouched, and so did hers. There was an ease to the conversation that surprised me—as if we'd skipped past the awkward introductions without needing to agree on it. At one point she smiled and said, almost casually, "I've been sitting behind you for weeks. You never turn around."

I laughed, embarrassed, realizing how much of the room I'd trained myself not to see.

Then, I felt the room register us. Conversations stalled. Heads turned. The sight of us together—talking, relaxed, and unguarded—had become a spectacle. My Black classmates stared openly, some with disbelief, others with expressions I couldn't yet read. White students noticed, too, though with a different, more detached curiosity. Nothing was said, nothing had to be. Amanda didn't flinch, and neither did I. For some reason, her certainty had already started to rub off on me.

Behind the counter, the women who ran the lunchroom caught my eye. One gave a slight nod; another smiled. It wasn't exactly approval—it was recognition. A quiet acknowledgment that a boundary had been crossed.

As the days passed, Amanda and I kept talking—between classes, in the hallways, and lingering after the bell when neither of us seemed in a hurry to go. She never explained why she'd written the notes, and I never asked. She didn't need to justify her interest for it to matter.

Through her, the things that had felt confusing about Rosenwald began to take shape. Amanda had been born at the Tyndall Air Force Base Hospital. One of her parents had served in the military before retiring in the Panama City area. Her family had traveled; they'd lived in more than one world. Panama City wasn't the center of her universe—it was simply where she was for now. That mattered. It explained her certainty about leaving. She talked about colleges up north the way some people talk about destinations they've already visited. Leaving wasn't a rebellion for her; it was a continuation.

In those conversations, the distance from my other Black classmates finally came into focus. It wasn't just indifference; it was caution spiked with resentment. I wore clothes that were in good repair. My shoes fit. Teachers learned my name quickly. I volunteered answers without worrying about who it might embarrass, and lunch money was never a concern. None of it was intentional, but all of it was visible. I was sending messages I hadn't meant to write.

Some classmates didn't have enough money for lunch. I watched the women behind the counter quietly fill trays for those who came up short, sometimes paying out of their own pockets. Other times, kids waited for leftovers, pretending they weren't hungry.

Seeing this made the air go thin around me. I talked about it with Amanda, but she didn't dramatize it. To her, poverty wasn't something to analyze—it was the air some people breathed. Ever-present. Managed. Endured. The realization embarrassed me. I'd spent weeks trying to understand the social distance without considering what I represented to them: mobility, judgment, and a reminder of options they didn't have. I hadn't chosen any of it, but I carried it anyway. Once I saw it, I couldn't unsee it.

Some kids had already resigned themselves by seventh grade—school a requirement before adulthood arrived with its predetermined limits. Others, like Amanda, clung to education as a way out. She wasn't waiting for permission to leave.

That knowledge changed how I moved through the halls. I listened more and spoke less. I raised my hand selectively. I began to understand that belonging wasn't just about being accepted—it was about not causing harm through my own obliviousness. I couldn't fix the systemic weight of the place, but I could stand differently. And sometimes, standing beside one person is enough to change the temperature of the whole room.

Chapter Twenty-Four

After three months at Treasure Cove Cottages, the military finally gave us a move-in date. A bedroom of my own at last. The news landed like a small miracle; boxes appeared, plans were made, and the countdown began.

Our joy lasted less than twenty-four hours.

That night, just before bedtime, Dad chained Heidi outside—our nightly ritual—to let her handle her business. She always barked when she was finished. Always. When she didn't, we assumed she was still sniffing around and kept watching television. Just before ten, Dad went to bring her in. He came back without her.

He called my name, and we grabbed flashlights. The night air was cool and the sky clear as we fanned out, calling her name again and again, our voices growing sharper with each pass. Nothing answered back. Then we heard it—a guttural, piercing scream that tore through the dark and froze us where we stood. It wasn't just a cry; it was something ripped from deep inside the body, raw and unfiltered. It broke into words only after the damage had been done

"No. No. No." Each one came heavier than the last.

Mom had found her.

Dad and I moved quickly, instinct pulling us forward. The beam of the flashlight dipped into the gutter, and there she was. Heidi's mangled body lay twisted along the edge of the highway, the asphalt slick with bright red blood shining beneath the streetlight. Whatever vehicle had struck her was long gone.

Karen burst through the front door, knowing the truth before her foot even hit the gravel. Dad caught her just in time, wrapping his arms around her with everything he had, physically keeping her from running into the street. I held Mom, turning her away, not letting her look any longer. She went limp in my arms. I don't remember crying; I only remember feeling hollow.

Dad borrowed a wheelbarrow and a shovel from the landlord. Together, we carried Heidi down toward East Bay and buried her that night, about fifty feet from the water's edge, behind the landlord's house on an otherwise beautiful, moonlit night. Dad drove the shovel into the ground again and again, harder each time, the rhythm steady and punishing. Watching him, I understood this was the only way he knew how to stand still. We finished in silence.

The next morning, our school bus rolled past Treasure Cove, right over the place where Heidi had been hit. The bloodstain was still there—dark, unmistakable. I stared at it as we passed. The stain stayed for weeks. Every day the bus crossed that stretch of road, I said nothing. I just looked, reliving the nightmare of that evening in my head.

We moved into our new house soon after. We would have other dogs during our time in Florida, but none of them replaced Heidi.

The person I worried about most after Karen was Dad. He was only three months removed from Vietnam, a place where he'd lost friends and where his work put him face-to-face with wounded and dying men every day. I didn't know what he had carried back with him. I hadn't asked—I'd been warned not to—but now he was in the position of consoling a grieving family when it should have been us helping him recover from his own ordeal.

I watched how little he slept, how he moved through the house at night, and how he stayed busy to keep from being still. He never mentioned Heidi again. I worried about him in ways I didn't yet know how to express. And like so many things in our house, that worry stayed unspoken.

Chapter Twenty-Five

The day after Heidi died, nothing at school looked different. The bells rang, lockers slammed, and teachers lectured. Rosenwald moved forward as if loss were a private inconvenience—something to be carried quietly and never acknowledged.

By lunch, my grief had settled into something heavier than sadness. It felt directional, pushing me toward a decision I hadn't yet named. Amanda found me in our usual corner. I told her what happened the night before; I didn't embellish, and I didn't need to. She listened without interrupting, then reached across the table and squeezed my hand. It was a small gesture, but it steadied me. Then she stood, walked around the table, sat beside me. She wiped the single tear on my cheek and kissed me right there. If I hadn't been grieving, I probably would've fainted.

Seconds later, the sound of a chair scraping against the floor broke the moment. Someone pulled out a seat on my other side. Her name was Rochelle. She was in my homework and pre-algebra class, but we'd never spoken. She slid into the empty spot as if it were the most natural thing in the world, smiled, and gave a nod to Amanda before looking at me. "How's your leg doing?" she asked.

The next day, another girl joined us. Then another.

By Wednesday, there were eight of us—me the only boy—laughing loud enough to draw looks from across the lunchroom. The jokes came fast, most of them at my expense. My New England accent became fair game; every carefully pronounced word earned a round of commentary. I welcomed it.

The conversation began to drift outward—to the places I'd lived, the schools I'd attended, and the simple fact that life could look different depending on where you landed. These weren't the same conversations I'd had with other military kids. We all traveled. We all moved. We all lived between assignments. But the kids at this table hadn't. Their questions weren't really about geography; they were about whether leaving was something people like them actually did. The outside world, I was learning, was an enigma to many of them.

By the end of the week, boys began drifting over—not the kids from the Air Force buses, but boys from the neighborhood. They didn't announce themselves; they just appeared, drawn by the noise and the girls. They didn't say much at first. They listened. They watched. They stayed.

Within ten days, the lonely table in the corner had transformed into a gathering place for twenty kids. All local. All carrying versions of the same reality. I did most of the talking at first—part habit, part nerves—but eventually, I learned when to step back and just listen. What formed there wasn't "integration" the way adults defined it. It wasn't a policy or a move toward progress. It was simply proximity.

Coach noticed before I ever said a word. One afternoon, he pulled me aside and told me what he'd been watching. He explained that the boys hadn't distrusted me personally; I simply represented something unfamiliar—mobility, options, and the idea that life didn't have to stop where it started.

"Be patient," he said, that wide-brimmed safari hat shadowing his eyes. "They'll come around."

Chapter Twenty-Six

The Mayflower truck pulled into our driveway the same day Rochelle joined our table at school. After eighteen months in storage, our furniture looked dusty and tired, but none of that mattered. Familiarity has its own gravity. The big brown sofa, Dad's Archie Bunker–esque recliner—pieces of a life we hadn't seen in over a year were finally back where they belonged. For the first time since arriving in Florida, something about our surroundings felt permanent.

I'd never had bedroom furniture of my own. We'd always borrowed whatever the military provided—whatever fit the assignment. Now there were boxes to open and decisions to make. Most of my toys hadn't survived the move, and old clothes, several sizes too small, were headed for the trash. I didn't miss them. I'd outgrown more than just fabric.

As the movers unloaded, kids hovered at the edges of the yard, measuring us. One by one, they drifted closer. A few were bold enough to introduce themselves to Dad first. That mattered; respect always mattered to him. To my surprise, he waved me in. I was allowed to mingle, as long as I stayed out of the way. To my surprise, he waved me in. I could mingle, as long as I stayed out of the way.

The questions came fast. *How old are you? What grade are you in? What sports do you play?* This was the interrogation Ms. Jones lite. A couple of kids recognized me from the bus, which instantly lowered the temperature. Within a week, I knew most of the neighborhood kids by name.

Our house sat on a massive corner lot—a single-story, three-bedroom square that felt cavernous after Treasure Cove. A giant tree dominated the front yard, its branches begging to be climbed. It quickly became the default meeting place for any kid looking to escape the sun. A long, meandering driveway led to a single-car carport and a semi-detached laundry room. My parents rushed out to buy a washer and dryer; we'd never owned our own before. Florida felt official now.

The front of the house featured a screened-in "Florida Room," partially hidden by thick brush. Like most military housing, the place was aggressively uninspired: square, utilitarian, and off-white. Across the street, the houses sat just ten feet from a dense forest that fed into East Bay. The woods were alive with things that slithered. Rattlesnakes loved the warm pavement. Mom thought one had found its way into our Florida Room, triggering a scream from Mom that I heard from half a mile away.

I arrived to find a small coral snake coiled in the corner, just as frightened as she was. A neighborhood kid helped me trap it in a box to carry it back to the woods. Dad had the screen fixed immediately. Mom was a city girl; to her, snakes belonged behind glass, preferably in a zoo.

The neighborhood sat on sand, and grass was more a suggestion than a reality. That became my problem. I inherited lawn duty. Eager to prove myself, I tried to get a head start before Dad could explain the mower. I poured oil into the gas tank and yanked the cord until sweat soaked my shirt. Nothing.

Dad stepped outside, already knowing something was wrong. I pointed to the tank. The pause was long enough to make me brace. His moods since Vietnam were growing more unpredictable—one minute volcanic, the next serene. This time, serenity won. He calmly drained the tank, refilled it properly, and pulled the cord. The mower sputtered to life, coughing out blue smoke as the oil burned away. Not a word was said. Mercy delivered.

By eight in the morning, the neighborhood hummed with mowers. By eleven, the ninety-degree heat turned punishing. I blacked out twice while cutting grass for neighbors, lucky to make it home both times. But the work paid—three dollars a yard, extra for hedges. It was my first steady income, and I loved the weight of my own money.

At six a.m. sharp, the first sortie announced itself, the F-106 Delta Darts rattling our windows and drowning out the morning news—an alarm clock only the military could justify.

The kids in the neighborhood came and went, but the Davidsons' house was the one that felt truly open. I drifted there naturally, welcomed without question. Joey Davidson became a fast friend, and in their house, I wasn't a guest; I was expected. I spent more sleepovers there than I can remember.

Wilson nearly fainted the first morning he saw me waiting at the new bus stop. He bolted off the bus and hugged me like I'd come back from the dead. I took my usual seat behind him, and we talked all the way to school. I had an address now. A place that didn't move. I could play ball in the street, ride my bike to the store, or just sit under the tree and do nothing at all.

School felt different, too. Not solved, but less brittle. Whatever this busing experiment was, it had started to grow roots. For the first time since we arrived, I felt anchored—still moving but no longer drifting.

Chapter Twenty-Seven

The neighborhood revealed itself in slow, simmering layers. During the day, it wore a mask of ordinary suburbia: the rhythmic drone of lawnmowers, kids weaving through the streets on bicycles, and the tinny hum of radios drifting through open garage doors. But at night, the Florida heat refused to dissipate. It lingered, thick and heavy, pressing against the houses until the walls seemed to sweat. In that damp stillness, conversations carried much farther than they should have. Despite the hum of air conditioners, many doors stayed propped open—the military, after all, picked up the electric bill—and voices drifted across property lines like a shared secret. You learned the intimate details of a neighbor's life without ever trying to.

Directly across the street lived the Whitfields. Like us, they were a Black military family, and they had a daughter my age named Samantha. She was a focused, exceptional student, always appearing with her head buried in a book, even during the chaotic, bumpy bus rides to Rosenwald. She had braces—a mechanical detail I'd soon be intimately familiar with—and a quiet, cute confidence that didn't demand attention but certainly commanded respect.

Yet, for the two years we lived as neighbors, I never truly got to know her. Samantha was a ghost in the midday sun. Her parents maintained a perimeter that was absolute: school to home, home to school. There were no bikes in the street for Samantha, no lingering on the sidewalk to chat, and no drifting toward the large, inviting tree in our yard where the other neighborhood kids gathered to kill time. She would remain inside her house until the school bus hissed to a stop exactly twenty feet from her door; only then would she sprint across the grass to board.

Her father was Captain Whitfield, a man of rigid posture and few wasted words. Her mother was a woman whose beauty and calm temperament mirrored my own mother's—precise, composed, and effortlessly elegant. When our parents crossed paths, they were friendly, their laughter easy and familiar. But Samantha remained just out of reach.

The longest conversation we ever had occurred one afternoon while I was playing catch with a friend behind her house. She pushed open her bedroom window, and we talked through the mesh of the screen for nearly an hour. It was a strange, filtered connection—a friendship mediated by wire and wood. I often wondered if it was the protective instinct for an only child or something deeper that kept her so strictly indoors, but from the safety of her room, she remained a mystery I was never allowed to solve.

Two doors down from the Whitfields lived the only other Black family in our hundred-home radius: the Jenkins.

If the Whitfield home was a sanctuary sealed by protection, the Jenkins house was a fortress ruled by force. The oldest son, Miles, was already in high school—a boy with the massive, terrifying frame of a middle linebacker. He had thick arms and shoulders that looked carved from stone, yet he possessed none of the aggression that usually accompanies such a build. He was polite, docile, and remarkably quiet. His younger brother was closer to my age, quicker to laugh but always looking over his shoulder.

Their father, Mr. Jenkins, was the most physically imposing human being I had ever encountered. He was a mountain of a man, pushing three hundred pounds, with a presence that sucked the oxygen out of a room. There was no ambiguity in that house; commands weren't discussed, they were issued like military decrees. It unsettled me to see a sixteen-year-old boy unable to cross the street without formal permission.

The first time I saw Mr. Jenkins strike Miles, the world seemed to tilt. It happened with a sickening speed—a disputed word, a sharp look, and then the heavy crack of a hand. No warning, no apology. Miles didn't protest; he simply absorbed the blow as if it were a scheduled part of his day.

It didn't stop there. Sometimes the violence happened in plain sight; other times, I would be pedaling my bike past their house and hear the muffled, dull punctuation of an impact followed by raised voices. I learned to pedal faster. I learned to look at my handlebars and pretend the wind was the only thing I heard. The fear crept inward, settling in my stomach like lead. My own father had a temper that could be volcanic, but it never crossed the line into physical cruelty. Mr. Jenkins lived on the other side of that line.

Eventually, the sheer weight of that house fractured our budding friendship. I stopped wandering over, and they stopped drifting down our driveway. I was learning that the neighborhood had borders you crossed at your own risk. Thankfully, the Davidsons lived right around the corner. They were white, and they didn't seem to care that I wasn't. Their home was the antithesis of the others—loud, messy, and entirely open.

I struggled to reconcile these three worlds. We lived on a military base—a gated, guarded, and orderly environment. The external threats that adults usually worried about didn't exist here in any way I could feel. Yet, the Whitfields and the Jenkins kept their children on a leash so tight it felt like a chokehold.

Years later, I would consider whether this was a direct, visceral response to the aftermath of the Civil Rights Movement. Down South, even behind the gates of a base, safety was a fragile concept, and fear was a silent inheritance. I realized then that my neighborhood wasn't just a collection of houses; it was a complex system of permissions. It dictated who could wander, who had to stay, and who was allowed to simply be a child.

At the time, I didn't know that Captain Whitfield was petitioning the school district to change the name of Rosenwald to honor a different Black historical figure. I didn't see the quiet battles he was fighting against a system that had denied the request. All I knew was that I was a boy looking for connection, and sometimes that connection was denied by caution, sometimes by control, and often without any explanation at all.

The real lessons weren't happening in Ms. Jones's classroom. They were being taught on the sidewalks and through the open windows of the Florida night. I was learning that proximity didn't guarantee access—and it never had.

Chapter Twenty-Eight

The invitation felt like a natural extension of a growing friendship. Joey Davidson asked if I'd been invited to Allison's thirteenth birthday party that Friday night. We shared several classes and talked often, usually about the grueling workload Ms. Jones and the other teachers piled on us. After all, we were seventh graders adjusting to a system of changing classes for each subject matter, one teacher not caring how much the other heaped on the work.

I hadn't received an invitation and wasn't particularly offended; I was still the new kid, and there was no reason for her to include me in her inner circle yet.

Joey, however, thought otherwise. He had a way of bulldozing through social nuances with the confidence of someone who had never been told "no." Somehow, he finagled an invite on my behalf, presenting it to me as a settled matter. I took the time to buy a card and a small gift, choosing it carefully at the base exchange, wanting to arrive with the right kind of etiquette. Joey's father drove us across the base, the cooling evening air rushing through the car windows. He dropped us at the curb with a cheerful "have a good time" before pulling away, leaving us in the flickering glow of the streetlights.

I felt entirely normal walking up to that door. I felt like a teenager, having just turned thirteen myself.

Then Allison's father answered.

The look on his face told me everything before his lips even moved. It was a look of instant, frozen recognition—the kind that categorizes a person before they can speak. He stepped forward just enough to block the doorway, his body language practiced, rigid, and final.

"You're not invited," he said. His voice was flat, devoid of the heat of anger, which somehow made it colder.

Joey tried to intervene, his voice rising in confusion as he insisted, he'd already cleared it with Allison. Her father didn't budge. He stood there like a sentry. It wasn't a discussion; it was a verdict handed down by a judge who had made up his mind years before I was born.

Behind him, I could see the party in full swing. Several classmates had gathered in the entryway, their laughter and the muffled beat of a radio spilling out onto the porch. A few called my name—confused at first, then falling into a heavy, awkward silence as they realized what was happening. Allison appeared in the hallway behind her father, her face pale, protesting weakly. It didn't matter. The door was a border, and I was on the wrong side of it.

I wasn't going in.

Joey began to object more loudly, his face reddening, but I reached out and pulled him away by the arm. I didn't want a scene. I didn't want to be the reason the music stopped. This wasn't Joey's fault, and I wasn't angry at him. I was simply hollowed out by the absolute certainty of the rejection. On the way back to the sidewalk, I passed a trash can. Without looking, I dropped the card and the gift into it. The "thud" it made against the plastic felt like a period at the end of a very long sentence.

After everything I'd been carrying since our arrival in Florida—the move, the school, the loss of Heidi—I didn't think it was possible to be hurt any more. I was wrong. The tears came without warning—hot, stinging, and deeply humiliating. I turned my face away from Joey, but there was no hiding the way my shoulders shook. Standing there on the sidewalk, dressed in my best clothes for a party I was forbidden to attend, I understood that all the quiet rejections and small exclusions of the past months had finally reached a breaking point.

The humiliation landed first, followed by a crushing sadness, and then something darker—a flicker of pure, crystalline rage. I thought briefly about retaliation—eggs, keyed cars, the small, jagged acts of revenge that thirteen-year-olds use to reclaim power. But that wasn't who I was. And more than that, I knew the shadow of my father. I knew what he would do if he found out I'd broken the law. Whatever momentary satisfaction vandalism offered wouldn't survive the volcanic consequence of his disappointment.

The beach sat less than half a mile away. I walked toward it, my dress shoes crunching on the sand and gravel until the houses thinned and the night opened up. The Gulf was a vast, dark mirror. Out on the water, shrimp boats moved quietly offshore, their green and red lights blinking like low-hanging stars. A sandbar called Shell Island shielded the harbor from the open Gulf, and I stood at the end of a small pier, watching the fishermen work in the rhythmic silence of the tide. They nodded at me—the kind of nod men give to other men when they see a weight being carried—and then returned to their nets.

Couples passed by barefoot in the sand, their low murmurs lost to the waves. I must have looked absurd—dressed up with nowhere to go, a boy in a costume for a life he wasn't allowed to lead. I bought a Coke from a rusted vending machine and sat on a weathered bench; the aluminum can freezing my hands. I turned over questions I didn't yet know how to phrase: *Would my friends still be my friends on Monday? Was this how the world worked—permission granted one minute, revoked the next?*

Around 9:30 p.m., I walked back toward Allison's house and sat on the curb, waiting for Joey's ride. One by one, the partygoers emerged. Each of them stopped to apologize, their voices soft and heavy with guilt. Their sincerity was real, but it didn't soften the bruise. Allison eventually came outside despite her father's orders, sitting beside me on the concrete in a quiet act of defiance. She offered an olive branch, but I wasn't ready to take it. The wound was still too raw, the air between us too thick with the things her father had said without speaking.

In the months that followed, I saw her father often on base. When other adults were around, he acted like we were old friends, flashing a plastic, professional smile. Every time, I felt a surge of that dark rage, wanting to slap the performance right off his face.

Joey told his father everything on the drive home. Mr. Davidson nearly turned the car around right then, cursing under his breath, his hands white-knuckled on the steering wheel. He was ready for a confrontation, but he caught my eye in the rearview mirror and thought better of it. He kept driving. I stayed silent, watching the dark Florida pines blur past.

When he dropped me off, he apologized again. He wanted to talk to my father—to explain. I stopped him. For all of my father's faults, being a coward wasn't one of them. If that conversation had happened, it would not have ended quietly, and I didn't want more violence. I wanted sleep.

My parents were in their bedroom when I got home. I called out a hollow "hello" and went straight to my room, closing the door on a world that suddenly felt much smaller.

For a few days, I withdrew into myself. I spoke only to the essentials: Joey, Amanda, and the small circle of Black friends at the corner table. But eventually, a quiet thirteen-year-old reckoning took place. I realized I wasn't being fair to the people who *did* want me there.

I received another invitation that same week. At first, I reflexively declined. Then I reconsidered on one condition: Kelly would need her parents' explicit permission. Not assumed. Not implied. Asked.

Her mother called our house herself. That night, I was welcomed without the slightest hesitation. Kelly's parents were unlike anyone I'd ever met—relaxed, funny, and dressed more like aging hippies than military officers. They hung around for an hour, acting as DJs and showing off dance moves that were surprisingly good for the times. The house felt easy. It felt safe.

Kelly and I became academic rivals, a friendly competition that pushed us both. A year later, her family transferred overseas, and like so many military connections, we lost touch. It was the rhythm of our lives.

I attended a few more parties after that, but I always insisted on that parental "okay." They became predictable affairs—couples pairing off in the shadows, music I didn't care for, and the occasional "token" invitation to a couple of Black girls so the hosts could feel they were doing the right thing. Eventually, the girls and I stopped showing up. We realized we didn't need an invitation to feel like we belonged to ourselves.

Chapter Twenty-Nine

June 1971 arrived quietly, drifting in on a stagnant breeze. School ended without ceremony, the sharp racial tensions that had greeted us in September now reduced to something faint and ever-present, like a layer of humidity you only stopped noticing because it never left. I should have felt a sense of liberation, but instead, the days stretched open—unstructured, silent, and deeply uncertain.

As the school buses stopped running, the geography of Bay County suddenly felt much larger. I found myself spending hours on the phone with Amanda, our conversations becoming a lifeline. She lived off-base, nearly fifteen miles from our house—a distance that rendered summer an impenetrable barrier unless a parent agreed to play chauffeur. None did. To make matters more complicated, she was headed to high school, entering a world of older peers and new pressures. Despite the logistics and the natural drift that usually follows such transitions, we stayed close through those early high school years, our voices tethered by a long-coiled phone cord and a shared understanding of what it meant to be "different" at Rosenwald.

Summer in the military is a season of disappearance. Orders come down like divine decrees; olive-drab moving trucks arrive, and goodbyes are rushed, utilitarian, and rarely dignified. The Jenkins family was gone by July, their house suddenly silent after months of muffled shouts. Joey Davidson left at the very start of vacation, his father retiring and moving the family back to Mississippi.

I stood in the driveway and watched the Davidsons pack, feeling a strange, heavy irony. In the years that followed, as I studied the history of the South, I would often wonder why a white Mississippi family had taken such a profound interest in me. Everything the world told me about Mississippi involved the assassination of Medgar Evers and a hardened, monolithic bigotry. Yet, the Davidsons had been my staunchest defenders. They were proof that the human heart doesn't always follow the map of its geography; in a place where integration was a law, they had practiced it as a matter of character. When their car finally pulled away toward the state that was supposed to hate me, I felt the small circle I'd built collapse inward.

Dad noticed the void.

One afternoon, he came home early, still in his crisp fatigue uniform, and told me to get in the car. There was no explanation, no father-son small talk. We drove in a thick silence until he pulled into a baseball field a few miles from home—a rough diamond carved out of sand and scrub, with chain-link fences that rattled in the salt breeze. He popped the trunk and handed me my glove and bat. He'd signed me up for Pony League, for thirteen- to sixteen-year-olds.

This would be the second time I'd played for a team called the Yankees. Even the uniforms were identical—those iconic pinstripes. It felt strangely circular, as if a piece of my old life in the North had successfully migrated south to find me. I didn't ask questions. I didn't hesitate. What mattered was that Dad had seen the emptiness of my summer and filled it with something solid and recognizable.

He introduced me to Coach Reader, who gathered the boys and announced the arrival of their newest teammate. The faces staring back at me were cautious and unreadable. Once again, I was the only Black kid in a sea of white faces, though I noticed other teams in the league had multiple Black players. Coach asked where I wanted to play.

"Center field," I said, "if possible."

I had my reasons. I was a good defensive player, tempered by the terrain. I'd spent countless hours in the sandy open spaces around our house tracking fly balls hit by older kids, learning how to adjust when the loose Florida ground shifted beneath my feet. Sand teaches you anticipation; you can't rely on a pure sprint because you'll slip. You have to read the ball's flight the moment it leaves the bat. You have to commit early.

Batting practice followed. It became a gauntlet for the new kid. The coaches were skeptical of my frame; I was six-foot-two and barely a hundred and forty-five pounds, yet I swung a thirty-four-ounce bat—heavy even by major league standards. It was far too much lumber for a boy my size, and the other kids laughed until I started making consistent, jarring contact. I sprayed line drives across the parched grass, the "crack" of the bat echoing off the empty bleachers. Eventually, they stopped laughing and just watched.

I started the season on the bench. With only ten players on the roster, I knew my chance would come, but for now, I sat with the coaches during the games. I found I enjoyed the perspective—talking strategy, timing the pitchers, and learning the tendencies of the opposing batters. In the top of the seventh inning of my first game, I finally took my place in center field. Seven innings only. No at-bats. No heroics. But standing there in those pinstripes, with the smell of oiled leather and dust in the air, something in me steadied.

That night, I slept in my uniform. I wasn't a little kid anymore, but I held onto that fabric as if it were an anchor. It smelled of sweat and ambition.

We lost that game. Then we lost again. And again. By the time I joined, the team was already 0-4; and we added three more loses to the tally. We simply weren't good; the only standout was Coach Reader's son, a talented player who would clearly go on to play college ball. I continued to sub in late—

right field one game, center another. Still no at-bats, but I didn't mind. I was a part of a roster. I was a name on a lineup card. For the moment, that was enough.

Chapter Thirty

It took four games before circumstances finally forced the issue. Only nine players showed up that afternoon, the humid Florida air hanging heavy over the dugout as we scanned the parking lot for late arrivals. None came. With no room to maneuver, Coach Reader didn't make a speech or offer a pep talk; he simply penciled my name into the lineup and handed me my glove. "You're in center," he said with a short nod.

I felt ready. Perhaps too ready. My heart hammered a steady, rhythmic pulse against my ribs as I jogged out to the grass.

The opposing pitcher was a kid named Donald, a few years my senior and already notorious throughout the league for a temper that sat just beneath the surface of his skin. We went to the same school, and I'd seen him lose his composure over missed calls and bad hops in the hallways and the gym. On the mound, he wasn't overpowering, but he was crafty. He threw a slow, deceptive fastball and possessed an assortment of off-speed pitches that seemed to hover in the air, baiting hitters into reaching and guessing.

By the sixth inning, the game was slipping away; we were down four to one. I'd walked once and struck out once, frustrated by the way his pitches looked like beach balls but moved like shadows. His fastball seemed to float—almost insultingly slow—yet it kissed the corners of the plate with a precision that felt personal.

In the bottom of the seventh, the final frame, something finally broke our way. A walk. A slow, dying roller to third that left everyone safe. Another walk. Suddenly, the bases were loaded, the tension in the stands rising like the heat off the asphalt.

I took my time walking to the plate. I deliberately borrowed the mannerisms I'd picked up from watching the greats on television—the way they knocked the dirt from their cleats, the slow, rhythmic waggle of the bat. It wasn't showy, just deliberate. I even jogged over to the third-base coach for instructions I didn't really need, just to settle my nerves and let Donald stew on the mound.

The first pitch came in soft and straight—Donald's version of a fastball. I watched it drift past the plate and snap into the catcher's mitt.

Strike one.

It barely made a sound. I stepped out of the box, shaking my head at the red Florida dust. He'd been throwing that same "nothing" pitch all game, and no one had made him pay for the arrogance of it.

I looked at the field. The coach wanted the ball hit to right, and I noticed the right fielder creeping in, shallow enough to share breath with the second baseman. They didn't think I could drive it. The alignment was an insult. I decided right then: if I saw that floaty fastball again, I was going to unload.

The next pitch was a carbon copy of the first. I torqued my hips and swung with everything my 145-pound frame could muster. The contact felt clean—not a "crack" so much as a solid, deep *thwack*. I started toward first, eyes tracked on the ball, assuming it would die somewhere short of the warning track.

The center fielder backpedaled. Then he turned and ran. Then he hit the fence.

The ball didn't stop. it sailed over the barricade and dropped into a thicket of brush just beyond the field of play. A grand slam.

The crowd erupted. Parents were on their feet, screaming into the afternoon sun, and my teammates spilled out of the dugout like a dam breaking. I rounded the bases in a state of quiet, ringing disbelief. The noise of the cheering faded until all I could hear was the frantic thud of my own breathing and the crunch of my cleats on the dirt.

As I rounded third, the path to home narrowed. My teammates, ecstatic and blind to the rules, had surged across the chalk line to meet me. I had to drift inward for a step—maybe two—to avoid colliding with them before correcting my course and stomping on home plate. I never even saw the line.

Back in the dugout, the atmosphere shifted instantly. The celebration died in our throats as we watched the coaches locked in a heated, low-voiced conversation with the home plate umpire. I started toward the bleachers, thinking of the postgame snacks, when Coach Reader stopped me, his hand on my shoulder.

"Have a seat son"

I sat. Coach knelt in the dust in front of me, his expression unreadable. He told me my run didn't count.

"Why?" I asked, my voice sharper and more defensive than I'd intended.

He explained it calmly, though I could see the frustration in his own eyes: I'd stepped inside the imaginary baseline. Even though the umpire had allowed my own teammates to block my path, the rule was the rule. My three RBIs counted—the runners I drove in were legal—and we still won the game. But my name wouldn't be on the scorecard for a home run.

I looked up. The umpire was standing near the backstop, watching me. He didn't look smug, but he didn't look sorry either. He gave a small, knowing smile, as if a complicated machine had just functioned exactly as he had designed it.

The parents went nuclear when the announcement hit the loudspeaker. People I'd never met were shouting at the umpire as he walked toward the parking lot. "How can you do that to a thirteen-year-old?" a woman yelled, her voice cracking with indignation.

A few days later, the universe provided a strange postscript. I ran into that same umpire in the restroom at the fields. He glanced at me while washing his hands, the water splashing loudly in the quiet room. He didn't apologize.

"Tough luck, kid," he said quietly, drying his hands. "I'll be watching you the rest of the year."

Then he walked out. I stood there alone, staring at my reflection in the spotted mirror, trying to understand what I'd done wrong—and wondering if "watching me" was a promise or a threat.

Chapter Thirty-One

The next game was against the powerhouse of our division. By then, we were no longer playing for standings; that ship had drifted over the horizon weeks earlier. We were playing for pride, for the comfort of routine, and for the simple, stubborn fact that the schedule said we had to show up. Only nine players reported to the dugout that afternoon. There was no bench, no margin for error, and no room for injury. If a single one of us came out of the game, we forfeited.

I started in center field, the pinstripes of my uniform already stained with the fine, red dust of the Florida panhandle. My first at-bat ended with a long, soaring fly ball to deep left—one of those hits that looks like a miracle off the bat until the air catches it and it dies on the warning track. I jogged back to the dugout disappointed but steady. I belonged out there now. I could feel it in the way I moved, the way I tracked the ball, the way the game had finally started to slow down for me.

My second at-bat came in the middle innings. The pitcher was sixteen, three years my senior and significantly broader. He was strong-armed and aggressive, the kind of player who used his velocity as a threat. The first pitch he threw sailed high and inside—so close I felt the distinct shift of air against my cheek. I stepped out of the box, adjusted my helmet with trembling fingers, and stepped back in.

The next pitch didn't miss. It struck my helmet just above the left ear hole.

The sound was violent and unmistakable—like a cinderblock cracking against a steel plate. It was a blunt, concussive thud that vibrated through the marrow of my skull and left my ears ringing with a high, piercing whistle. For a moment, the world simply tilted. My helmet launched toward the backstop, a plastic shell unable to contain the impact, and my legs gave way. I hit the dirt hard, the taste of copper in my mouth.

Players from both teams sprinted toward the plate. Coaches ran, and classmates poured out of the bleachers in a wave of sudden, sharp concern. Hands reached down to me; voices stacked on top of each other, all asking the same frantic questions. Everyone moved except the umpire. He stayed exactly where he was, a silent statue behind the catcher, watching the chaos with a detached, clinical indifference.

I got to one knee, dizzy but conscious, blinking through the noise as teammates helped me up. Coach Reader was already yelling from the dugout as he ran to the field to check on me, his voice sharp with urgency and anger. The umpire still said and did nothing.

I managed to get to one knee, dizzy and blinking through the blurred noise as my teammates helped me to my feet. Coach Reader was already halfway across the diamond, his voice sharp with a mixture of urgency and burgeoning anger. The umpire still said nothing. He didn't check on me; he didn't warn the pitcher. He simply pointed toward first base. I took the bag, my head thumping with every step.

The following inning, it happened again. A pitch rode behind me; a clear message sent in a language I was beginning to understand all too well. Another close call, and still, the umpire offered no protection. Coach Reader left the dugout this time, crossing the field toward the opposing bench. His hands were out, his voice raised—not in a threat, but in an urgent plea to stop the escalation before something worse happened. The umpire finally intervened, looking more irritated by the delay than concerned for the players. I stayed in the game because there was no alternative. We had no ten.

In the sixth inning, I came up again. We were well behind by then, the outcome of the game a foregone conclusion. The first pitch buzzed past my back, close enough to graze my jersey. The second slammed directly into my left forearm, just above the wrist.

The pain was immediate, white-hot, and absolute. I dropped to the dirt, clutching my arm as the skin began to swell and discolor before my eyes. I knew the sensation of breaking; I knew immediately I'd be headed to the emergency room.

This time, the fragile order of the afternoon shattered. Parents in the stands began shouting, the sound echoing off the metal bleachers. Someone actually vaulted the fence. The pitcher—the same kid I'd hit the home run off weeks earlier, a classmate from Rosenwald—was actually crying as he reached down to help me up. His teammates followed, surrounding me in a circle that felt protective, almost apologetic. It took several minutes of shouting and gesturing for the adults to restore a semblance of order.

Coach Reader wanted me out. He said it plainly, his face pale. But the math hadn't changed: we still only had nine players. If I sat, my teammates lost. I told him I could stay. He looked at my arm—already stiffening, the bone screaming beneath the skin—and hesitated. Then he nodded. In that moment, there were no good choices, only the least bad one.

A teammate helped force my glove onto my left hand, hiding the grimace on my face from the coaches' view. I jogged back to center field, cradling my arm, pretending the world wasn't throbbing in time with my heart. The very next batter hit a high, lazy fly ball straight to me. I took one step to my right and waited, neck craned upward, tracking the white speck against the fading blue sky. When the ball finally landed in the pocket of my glove, a bolt of agony shot from my forearm to my shoulder like a live wire. I held on.

Dad arrived just as the game ended, finding me standing on first base after my final at-bat. The people in the stands didn't realize he was my father, or the air in the park might have shifted sooner. Coach Reader spotted him and left the dugout for a quick, hushed chat. From my place on the bag, I could read Dad's body language with perfect clarity. He wasn't just concerned. He was dangerous.

Trouble was brewing; it had arrived.

Dad went after the opposing coach, his voice a roar, spitting words and accusations I'd never heard him use before. It was the volcanic side of his post-Vietnam temper, raw and terrifying. It took four grown men to hold him back, and in the struggle, the seams of his uniform literally tore. Someone in the crowd threatened to call the police.

An hour later, the cold clinical lights of the ER and the subsequent X-rays confirmed the fracture. It was a clean break, but a painful one. Another cast. More weeks of being "the kid with the plaster."

That was the end of baseball for me. I never played organized ball again. Whatever joy the game once held—the rhythm of the pinstripes, the smell of the grass—vanished in the space of those six innings. Dad tried later with coaching, encouragement, and appeals to nostalgia, but I wouldn't budge. My relationship with the game was dead.

All I knew was that for the second time in less than six months, a white adult male in a position of "neutral" authority had exercised that power in a way that left no room for appeal, no protection, and no recourse. The lesson was clear: surrender yourself to their authority and hope they decide to be kind. It was a lesson I would spend the rest of my life trying to course-correct.

Chapter Thirty-Two

September 1971

Riding the bus to Rosenwald for eighth grade felt fundamentally different than the year before. The ambient fear that had defined my seventh-grade mornings was still there, but it belonged to someone else now. The new students—white kids being bused into the neighborhood for the first time—carried the same rigid tension I had worn the previous fall. Their shoulders were tight, their eyes darting and alert, treating every bump in the road like a potential ambush.

On those long rides, someone always tried to break the stifling tension, and usually, it happened through song. One of the older kids would start softly, testing the air, and before long the entire bus would swell into a rolling choir. The songs leaned heavily anti-war, their lyrics floating above us like a dare. Country Joe and the Fish became a regular anthem:

And it's one, two, three, what are we fighting for...

We sang it loudly and with a strange confidence, as if none of our fathers wore the uniforms of the very machine we were mocking—as if none of them had just returned from Vietnam or were quietly bracing to head back. The contradiction was thick, but as teenagers, we breathed it without choking.

That year, Don McLean's "American Pie" arrived, its eight-minute sprawl turning the bus into a nightly revival. No one truly understood what the "levee" or the "jester" meant, but it didn't matter. The song had a communal gravity that held our disparate lives together for the duration of the ride.

The white kids leaned hard into the burgeoning hippie culture—long hair, deliberately unwashed jeans with frayed hems, and peace signs dangling from every neck and jacket. Their rebellion was loud, aesthetic, and colorful. I, however, found myself gravitating toward a different rhythm. Black style spoke to me with a clarity the hippie movement lacked. I embraced the bell-bottoms that finally provided cover for my oversized feet and a hairstyle that refused any form of discipline.

I hadn't committed to a full Afro yet, mostly because my hair was stubborn. I soon realized my "good hair" was biologically opposed to the perfect sphere of an Afro, no matter how much product I jammed into it.

Dad, ever the military man, tried to fight the times. He attempted to transform me into a clean-cut kid, using everything from stocking caps and Brylcreem to the jagged, unforgiving shears of military barbers—the latter of which always drew Mom's sharp ire. He even tried to cut it himself once, leaving me with a mane that looked like a tragic cross between a troll doll and boxing promoter Don King. Girls—both Black and white—tried their hand at braiding it, but nothing held. Eventually, I surrendered, letting my hair do exactly what it wanted.

We sang about peace while the nightly news was a montage of fire. The ghosts of Kent State—four students dead in thirteen seconds—still hovered in the back of our minds. We knew that in a few short years, we'd be draft-eligible ourselves, a reality that kept Dad awake at night even if it didn't bother me yet. Fortunately, we were thrown a draft "lifeline" about a year later that changed the stakes for all of us.

When we arrived at Rosenwald that first morning, class didn't start with the usual bell-regulated coldness. Instead, the school turned into a massive, joyous reunion. Kids hugged in the hallways; teachers lingered in doorways to trade jokes; music echoed off the lockers. Even when the bell finally rang, no one moved—not even the faculty. The distance that had defined the previous year had collapsed. Black and white students talked with an ease that would have been unimaginable twelve months prior. I noticed it in the small, human gestures: who stood close, who laughed without looking over their shoulder, who touched a classmate's arm mid-sentence.

"Benneeeeeett!"

I stepped into the gym and Coach Collier made a beeline for me, bypassing a dozen other students in something close to a sprint. He greeted me with a bear hug that nearly cracked my ribs. In that moment, I realized Rosenwald had become a place of safety for me. Amanda was gone—off to high school—but I no longer needed a protector to survive the day. I had grown into the space.

Then lunch arrived, and with it, a cold dose of reality. Many of my Black friends didn't eat—not that day, and not most days. In the economy of the schoolyard, a single dollar might as well have been a hundred. I began lending money, though it was less of a loan and more of a quiet tithing. When a classmate asked to "hold a dollar," I knew it was a gift I'd never see again. Eventually, someone reported my "banking operations" to the administration, and they shut me down. I complied briefly, then reopened quietly. Hunger at that scale was impossible to ignore. There were programs, supposedly, but my friends always seemed to fall just outside the margins of paperwork and pride.

The social landscape was shifting in other ways, too. The girls were changing—or perhaps I was finally paying attention. They were filling out in ways that reminded me of the sights at Panama City Beach, and the trend of the day—bra-less halter tops didn't exactly help my concentration. This newfound freedom gave them a confidence that bordered on the revolutionary. We held hands, walked the white sands of the beaches, and went to the movies—and we paid the "social tax" for it. Police calls, matches flicked at my face, fake guns pulled as "warnings," and slurs delivered with casual, smiling confidence. Some parents bristled, but I drew my strength from the girls who refused to retreat, even though they didn't have to carry the specific weights of being me.

* * *

With baseball forever in my rearview mirror, I returned to another one of my early loves: bowling. Tyndall Lanes became my true refuge. The youth bowling program was run by Gladys, a woman who was stern, watchful, and entirely unimpressed by teenage tantrums. I was hyper-competitive; when a shot didn't break or bad luck left a pin standing, I burned hot. I slammed equipment and cursed under my breath until Gladys stepped in.

She didn't scold me; she monitored the fire. She started asking real questions—about home, school, and the things I was bottling up. She made sure my passion didn't turn into a forest fire. Eventually, once I proved I could control my temperament, she trusted me with real responsibility. By the end of the season, my average had skyrocketed, placing me among the elite bowlers not just on the base, but across the entire Panama City area.

I became someone the younger kids watched and mimicked. I wasn't appointed to lead, but I was reachable. Soon, parents were approaching me for "bowling wisdom." *"Michael, can you tell Jeri to slow down? Michael, Peter keeps dropping his shoulder, can you talk to him?"* As the fall season marched on, I became "Coach Bennett." For the first time, I felt truly needed. I would sit in my room at night devising lessons, even role-playing how I'd reach an ill-tempered child—essentially, how I'd reach a younger version of myself. Gladys saw me in action and eventually turned over the entire youth league (ages 5–11) to me, a fourteen-year-old.

Suddenly, adults were calling our house to discuss their children's success. Those conversations often morphed into something deeper—genuine peer-to-peer friendships. Older people made room for me at their tables. They treated me like a "big brother" to their kids and a friend to themselves; if I'd been of age, they likely would have taken me out for a drink. I had so many dinner invitations that I barely ate at home.

I relished the adult-like conversations. Perhaps I was growing up too soon, faster than my parents were ready for. But conversation with other adults was a vital piece of education about the world that Mom and Dad had tried to shield me from.

I started hanging out at the lanes on school nights, often hitching rides home with adults who wouldn't bring me back until 11 p.m. In the quiet of those car rides, I asked the questions my parents wouldn't address—about girls, about racism, and about the world outside the gates. One even offered unsolicited advice on how to deal with someone traumatized by Vietnam. I listened, realizing that while I was teaching kids how to bowl, the world was finally teaching me how to navigate the men who had come home from the war.

Chapter Thirty-Three

I had entered what a parent once aptly called the "ugly stage"—that awkward, jagged stretch of adolescence where your body seems to betray you on a daily basis.

My permanent teeth had arrived long before my face had grown enough to host them. They looked oversized and aggressive, some still trapped beneath swollen, tender gums that pushed my lips forward into a permanent pout. Others grew at rebellious angles, as if they were trying to escape my jaw rather than align with it. The mirror became a daily adversary. At fourteen, smiling wasn't a natural reaction; it was a calculated strategy.

My parents decided medical intervention was the only solution. Dr. Johnson's orthodontic office was located on Harrison Avenue, the main artery of Panama City. Everything of consequence—whether ordinary or infamous—seemed to happen on that stretch of road. It housed the local Sears and the town's solitary McDonald's, but it was also the same pavement where my parents had once witnessed the chilling spectacle of a Ku Klux Klan rally. Harrison Avenue didn't discriminate between the mundane and the obscene; it simply hosted both under the same flat Florida sun.

Dad arrived at Rosenwald mid-morning to sign me out for an appointment. The school's intercom system was down, which forced him to wait in the main hall while a student was dispatched to find me. I spotted him from the far end of the corridor before he saw me, and I immediately noticed the way the atmosphere in the hallway changed.

Heads turned. Stares lingered. I didn't understand the sudden shift at first, but then I tried to see him the way my classmates did—tall, composed, and light-skinned, with features that defied easy categorization. To me, he was just Dad, the man who fixed the lawnmower and lost his temper over baseball. To the students at Rosenwald, he was a walking interrogation.

The questions didn't start until gym class the following day. At first, they sounded casual, almost like jokes, but they quickly sharpened until they were drawing blood.

"Why didn't you tell us your daddy was white?"

The names followed, stacked on top of one another like punches: *Cracker. Honky. White boy. Uncle Tom.* It was an hour-long interrogation disguised as locker-room banter. The reaction wasn't a slow build; it was an unleashed torrent. The information of my lineage had been there all along but seeing him in the flesh had given everyone permission to vocalize their suspicions.

Most of my white classmates already knew Dad, or at least knew of him through the base, so they didn't make a scene. But the reaction from my Black peers cut much deeper. The revelation didn't just create tension; it exposed a fracture that had been hiding beneath the surface of our recently improved relationship. I'd been blinded by how well things had been going at the lunch table, and in my naivety, I hadn't anticipated the fallout. It wasn't my first time dealing with this, but it felt like a regression

That afternoon, flag football crossed an invisible line. Elbows landed high against my ribs; hands struck low. High-top cleats found my knees, which everyone knew were already vulnerable from previous injuries. Everything stayed just "legal" enough for the coaches to ignore, but I went home that day bruised in places I couldn't easily explain to my mother.

After class, the questions returned—lower, slower, and more deliberate. Why hadn't I mentioned it? What else was I keeping to myself? I felt as though I owed them a ledger of my history just to prove I belonged. I gave them what I had: stories of Grandma Jean, our family history in the North, and the mystery of Dad's own biological father. But speculation always fills the gaps where facts are thin.

For the first time, I understood a lesson that wasn't in any textbook: inside the Black community, "shade" could fracture trust in an instant. Outside of it, my appearance made people hesitate, unsure of which social box to shove me into. My father's appearance didn't grant me the "white privilege" some of my peers assumed it did. It didn't protect me from slurs or quiet the police calls.

A month later, both of my parents signed me out together for a follow-up appointment. This time, the reaction was the polar opposite. Mom's beauty drew immediate, vocal admiration—whistles and comments that crossed lines I wasn't willing to let stand. I corrected a few boys physically, without apology, and the "cold shoulder" from the previous month vanished overnight. Acceptance returned as if the interrogation had never happened.

So, this was the social math of my life: one parent complicated me, while the other clarified me. I began to understand, dimly and imperfectly, the duality my father must have lived with decades earlier—the simultaneous inclusion and exclusion, the doors that were half-open and half-slammed. You never truly knew which version of yourself the person across from you was seeing. The "ugly stage" wasn't just about my teeth; it was about realizing how fragile belonging actually was, and how quickly it could be revoked based on nothing more than a glance.

Chapter Thirty-Four

By the time the orthodontic work began in earnest, I was already internalizing a lesson no one had taught me directly: some pain was simply expected, and complaining about it only made the burden heavier.

The braces were the most visible sign of the "renovation," but the palate expander was the true architect of my discomfort. It was a rigid metal bar anchored to my upper molars, cemented into place like rebar holding together a brick wall. Once a day, I was required to perform a grim ritual: I had to insert a small metal pin—no thicker than a paperclip—into a tiny hole at the center of the device and turn it.

Each turn applied a deliberate, mechanical pressure designed to literally widen my upper jaw so the teeth still trapped beneath my gums could eventually drop into place. You could feel the gears of your own skull shifting immediately. A deep, spreading pressure radiated upward through my face, into my sinuses, and behind my eyes. My jaw would throb for hours afterward, a dull ache settling in like something permanent. I learned to do it at night, right before bed, so I wouldn't have to speak to anyone while my face felt like it was being pried apart from the inside.

Six months into the process, the gap between my two front teeth had grown so wide it became a form of public entertainment. My classmates treated it like a scientific oddity. They measured the distance and posted the "results" on my locker door like game scores. One kid even brought a roll of quarters to school and proudly demonstrated that at least six of them could fit cleanly in the canyon between my teeth. I laughed when it was expected of me, but mostly I kept my mouth shut.

Smiling had become a calculated act of vulnerability I wasn't always willing to risk.

The pain behind my eyes, the constant throb in my jaw, and the knees that never quite forgot the humidity—discomfort had become my routine. It was a masterclass in pain management without medication.

Gym class was supposed to be where effort turned into strength—where movement meant freedom. For me, it became the place where all of that collided.

Gym class was supposed to be the arena where effort turned into strength, but for me, it was where all my physical limitations collided. Coach Collier had always been my protector; he understood the reality of my Osgood-Schlatter disease and the flare-ups that arrived without warning. On most days, he watched me with a fatherly eye, pulling me aside when I needed a break.

But one morning, that protective balance shattered. Someone had stuffed a rag into a locker room sink and left the water running—a mindless prank that resulted in a flood seeping into the newly resurfaced gym floor. For a school like Rosenwald, which measured every dollar twice, the damage to the floor was a minor catastrophe. No one confessed, and Coach finally snapped.

We ran. First sprints, then more sprints, then grueling distance laps. The whistle cut through the humid air relentlessly, allowing just enough time to catch a breath before we were ordered back to our feet. It wasn't discipline anymore; it was an outpouring of fury.

I tried to keep up, my lungs burning, until halfway through a lap, my left knee simply gave out. There was no drama to the fall—no shout, no cinematic collapse. The joint just stopped responding to my brain's commands. I went down hard on the track, the familiar, white-hot pain surging through my leg like an electrical current. I stayed there in the dirt, my jaw clenched so tight I thought my braces might shatter, waiting for the world to stop spinning.

Coach ordered me to stand. I couldn't.

For a heartbeat, it looked like he might lose his temper with me, too—until an assistant coach stepped in, quietly reminding him of my diagnosis. A few students helped me off the track and sat me on the grass. Coach barked at them to get back in line and finish the punishment, and I watched the rest of the class run while the sweat dried on my skin and my knee pulsed with a steady, rhythmic agony. I didn't say a single word.

Later that morning, while walking to second period, the knee buckled again. My books hit the hard tile floor with a loud, echoing thump, and I let out an earth-shattering scream as I hit the ground knee-first. I folded my hands over the joint, rocking back and forth on the floor as if I could physically push the pain away.

Two teachers rushed to me, and several students carried me to the nurse's office, my arms draped over their shoulders as if I were an injured player being taken off the field on a Sunday afternoon. The nurse listened as I explained the orthopedist's instructions, then asked if I'd done anything strenuous in gym.

I lied. Coach Collier was like a second father to me, and I wasn't about to be the reason he faced a disciplinary board.

But word reached him anyway. He pulled me out of class later that day, his voice quieter and more somber than I'd ever heard it. He apologized fully and sincerely, his eyes welling with enough regret that I knew he meant it. I told him I was fine, which was an obvious lie, but one we both needed to believe.

He excused me from gym for two weeks. Then, in an act of incredible character, he called my father to explain exactly what had happened. Dad didn't get angry at the Coach. In his mind, "toughening me up" wasn't cruelty; it was the only way to prepare a young man for a world that wouldn't care about his knees.

By then, the pain had stopped announcing itself with such violence. It just settled in—a dull, reliable ache below the kneecaps that was ever-present but no longer debilitating. I stopped talking about it. What was the point?

Explaining symptoms to my father was like hitting my head against a brick wall. He often boasted that he'd never suffered a real injury in his life, conveniently forgetting the time in Spain when he ran with the bulls and one caught him in the thigh, tossing him ten rows into the stands. The alcohol he'd consumed that day had likely dulled the pain of the twenty stitches and the deep gash that nearly severed his leg. That wound had healed; my knees, however, would be a constant for the next fifteen years.

Chapter Thirty-Five

I didn't join the track team because Coach asked me to. I joined because, despite everything that had changed for the better at Rosenwald, I still wasn't fully inside the circle.

By the spring of eighth grade, I had real friends across racial lines. I laughed in the hallways and had a permanent seat at the lunch table. But among a specific, influential group of my Black peers, I remained "the other." I was tolerated and occasionally respected for my grades or my wit, but I was rarely truly embraced. I wanted what they had with each other—that effortless, shorthand brotherhood. I wanted to be "one of the guys."

At Rosenwald, sports operated as the primary currency of social standing. If you played, you mattered; your presence carried weight. If you didn't, you hovered on the margins, no matter how smart, funny, or loyal you were. Coach didn't need to convince me to run. He simply opened a door I was already leaning against with all my might.

Track felt like my last, best chance at total immersion. I was willing to ignore the throbbing in my knees to fit in—willing to strike a dangerous bargain with my own body if it meant the prize was belonging. I also knew, in that quiet place where ego meets observation, that I was the best athlete left in the school who wasn't already committed to a jersey. That knowledge gave me a flicker of confidence, even as the old familiar doubts worked at my resolve from the inside.

Running asked for something refreshingly simple: show up, endure, and don't quit. After the bureaucratic heartbreak of baseball, that simplicity felt honest.

I wasn't built for the explosive, violent bursts of the sprinters—those guys who joked about Jesse Owens and talked about the wind parting their Afros. I was long, thin, and angled, better suited for leverage and sustained momentum than raw twitch-speed. The mile became my event. So did the quarter-mile—a brutal, exposed race that is too long to fake and too short to hide.

Running stripped everything away. There was no room for posturing once your quadriceps turned to stone and your lungs felt like they were filled with hot glass. The body doesn't care who accepts you when oxygen becomes scarce; it only cares if you can make the next turn.

Before the season officially started, Mom forced Dad to take me back to the orthopedist to see if modern medicine could fortify my crumbling knees. We settled on elastic knee braces. The constant, firm pressure they applied to the tendons just below my kneecaps felt like a permanent deep-tissue massage, providing a much-needed sense of stability. The elasticity allowed my knees to bend, but only to a point, which made a true "kick" at the finish line nearly impossible. But they allowed me to compete, and at fourteen, that was the only victory I required.

I never won a single race. I finished second four times in the mile and lost badly more than once—so badly that I measured the gap between me and the leader in minutes rather than seconds. After those crushing defeats, I would lie flat on the sun-baked rubber of the track, staring up at the vast Florida sky while my chest heaved and my vision narrowed into a dark tunnel. I'd ask myself why I kept doing this.

But somewhere between the losses and the near-misses, I earned something far more durable than a plastic trophy. I earned proximity. I earned credibility. I found a place close enough to belonging that, for a while, it felt entirely real.

The bus rides to the meets at Tommy Oliver Stadium mattered more than the races themselves. That was where the social shift actually happened. We'd pile onto the bus, knees jammed into the vinyl seat backs, our bodies still buzzing from the adrenaline of warm-ups. Someone always brought a cassette player or an eight-track, and the music would rotate through soul, rock, and R&B—whatever someone had "borrowed" from an older sibling. Nobody cared about the color of the sound as long as the beat hit right.

The jokes came fast and jagged. *"Yo mama so ugly her pillow cried when she went to sleep." "Yo mama so ugly her shadow quit."* We laughed until our ribs ached. The trash talk flew in every direction, but it stayed playful—a linguistic sparring match that bridged the gap between the base and the neighborhood.

This was a mixed-race team, and somehow, in the cramped confines of that bus, we'd figured it out. We knew how to joke without cutting and how to push without breaking. Sweat leveled the playing field; fatigue erased the hierarchy. Sitting together on the grass between events, stretching and waiting our turn, I finally felt the one thing I'd been chasing since we crossed the Florida line.

I belonged.

Coach Collier never pretended I was a superstar. He didn't push me past what my braces could handle. He listened when I spoke, adjusted the workouts, and let me swap out long jogs for the specific physical therapy exercises my doctor had designed. To my surprise, other kids started following my routine, mimicking my stretches as if I were a veteran.

Somewhere along the way, running stopped being solely about social acceptance and became a quest for control. I couldn't control biased umpires. I couldn't control the deep-seated bigotry of a stranger. I couldn't control how authority figures bent the rules to suit their whims. But on that track, I could control my pace. I could control my breath. I decided when to push and when to back off.

I was learning that retreat wasn't always a sign of weakness; sometimes, it was a strategy for survival.

Track didn't demand the kind of physical confrontation that baseball had forced into the open. it allowed me to postpone a reckoning I wasn't quite ready for—the truth that some people in this world would hurt you simply because they possessed the power to do so. I didn't know it yet, but something heavier was on the horizon, something that wouldn't allow for lanes or distance. Something that required collision and a final, definitive choice.

Track taught me how to run toward acceptance. Soon, I'd have to decide if running was enough to keep me whole.

Chapter Thirty-Six

By the time I reached the end of eighth grade, something had shifted within me that no report card could measure. I was still a "good student"—efficient and restless—but my curiosity had turned sharper. I wasn't just absorbing information; I was interrogating it. The problem was systemic: I had questions the world wasn't prepared to answer, and no teachers were assigned to handle them.

School offered facts neatly boxed, like specimens in a lab. Timelines ended conveniently at the Civil War; Reconstruction was a mere paragraph, and Jim Crow a footnote. Slavery was presented as something that simply *ended*, not an institution that evolved. Whatever had shaped the air of Panama City remained unspoken.

I felt that absence like the heavy humidity before a storm. I saw it in the way older Black men avoided eye contact with white strangers, and in the raw poverty off-base that stood in such stark contrast to the insulated military cocoon. No one explained how both worlds could exist on opposite sides of the same fence. At Rosenwald, history felt sealed behind glass—dates and names without the connective tissue of why the South still felt like an unhealed wound.

So, I started asking. I questioned teachers, classmates, and neighbors, quickly becoming a royal pain in the ass. *Why were so many Black families still trapped in poverty? Why did authority figures operate by rules that shifted depending on who stood at the plate?* Most adults responded with discomfort. "You'll understand when you're older," they'd say, or "Don't dwell on it." Once, when I pushed a history teacher on the mechanics of busing, he told me flatly that "now was not the time." My retort—asking when that time would be—earned me a sharp reprimand.

But I *was* older. I was old enough to notice contradictions and feel an anger I had no place to put. I turned to the Tyndall library, checking out college texts and dense histories I barely understood on the first pass, rereading pages until the ink blurred. Even at the orthodontist, I ignored the comic books for *Time* or *Newsweek*. The receptionist once asked why a boy my age wanted to read those instead of "appropriate" material. I had no answer; I just knew I was looking for a truth not offered in class.

The *Panama City News Herald* arrived daily. In Maine, I'd only read the sports, but now I started with the front page. Dad, a news junkie who watched the nightly broadcast for military promotion requirements, finally found common ground with me. He wanted to climb the ladder; I wanted to know why the ladder was built this way. This thirst allowed me to hold my own with adult friends at the bowling alley, feeding them information they'd missed.

Ultimately, I realized that no one was responsible for filling in the gaps. Teachers taught what was assigned; parents carried unhealed scars; institutions protected themselves. The burden of connecting the dots fell to kids like me. Ignorance wasn't accidental; it was curated. Real knowledge came at a cost—the cost of my own comfort. I lost my innocence question, by question, realizing that fairness wasn't a guarantee written into law; it was something that had to be recognized, demanded, and eventually, fought for.

Chapter Thirty-Seven

I wasn't looking forward to the summer of 1972. Like the year before, the neighborhood began to hollow out almost immediately—orders came down, moving trucks appeared, and houses emptied. Despite Dad's persistent suggestions, baseball was out of the question; I'd made that boundary clear. I also had no interest in another summer spent cutting grass in the miserable Florida heat for embarrassing wages.

Dad, ever the pragmatist, came up with an alternative. "Let me see if I can get you a job bagging groceries at the commissary—the tips are great."

My response surprised him. "No way. I'm not working for tips."

That annoyed him, so he pivoted to the bottom line. "You could make forty, fifty dollars a day."

That got my attention. The commissary was the military's discounted grocery store, a vital perk for service members whose wages barely stretched to the end of the month. On the first and fifteenth—military paydays—the place was a gauntlet of shoppers. A fast bagger could pull in a hundred dollars or more on those days. In 1972, that was a fortune for a fourteen-year-old.

Dad made it happen without a single sheet of formal paperwork. Approval rested entirely with two men who controlled the bagging roster: the store manager and the grocery manager. Both were named Larry. Together, they ran the world of the commissary.

I didn't meet them initially; Dad handled the arrangements, which likely explained the startled looks I received on my first day. I was the only Black bagger in the store. I worked hard, kept my head down, and learned the frantic rhythm of the checkout lanes. I was polite, efficient, and reliable, earning the respect of the cashiers and the active-duty military guys who bagged part-time for extra cash.

After a few weeks, however, the "Larrys" issued an order to cut my hours. A few days later, my shifts were slashed again. No explanation was offered. The active-duty guys noticed the pattern before I did; they understood the silent politics of favored shifts. In a quiet show of solidarity, a couple of them rearranged their own schedules to keep me working, and one even handed over a prime payday shift so I wouldn't lose out on the top tips.

Despite their help, I was fired a week later. Again, no explanation. At fourteen, I was blindsided and didn't know how to advocate for myself, so I went home and waited for Dad.

When he heard what happened, he didn't ask for a play-by-play. He grabbed his keys, and we drove straight back to the commissary. He told me to wait outside the office. I never asked what was said behind that closed door, but I remember how the muffled, heated tones leaked through the walls. I know how long that door stayed shut, and I know exactly how it ended.

The two Larrys were relics of a vanishing era, much like the old guard at the bowling alley. They were the kind of men who would smile to your face while looking for a place to slide the knife. By then, I'd been in the South for over two years, and this "outward politeness masking inward malice" had become a constant in my lived experience. They operated under the delusion that they were smarter than the people they were trying to marginalize. They fooled no one—least of all a father who refused to back down, and a son who was busy learning how to do the same.

I was rehired on the spot and by mid-August, I'd saved well over a thousand dollars, opening my first bank account.

Chapter Thirty-Eight

August 1972

The sun dipped low behind the horizon, bleeding jagged streaks of red, orange, and yellow across the western Florida sky. I stood perfectly still on the parched grass, helmet in hand, watching as my teammates drifted like ghosts toward the locker room.

Our first day of football practice was over, but the air still felt thick with the day's heat and a strange, unsettled tension. The world felt unsteady, as if it were inching toward something violent and unavoidable. The news had trained us for that—Vietnam, Cambodia, Northern Ireland—it was a steady drumbeat of global fracture.

The Summer Olympics were in full swing, and I couldn't wait to get home to reconvene with Dad in front of the television. He met me at the door, having just turned the set off. His face was grave. Several Israeli athletes had been taken hostage, and he wanted to explain the stakes before I saw the images for myself. We turned the TV back on to non-stop coverage of what would become the Munich Massacre. I missed Jim McKay's famous, heartbreaking announcement—*"They're all gone"*—but Dad gave me the cliff notes. He looked at me then, his eyes searching mine. "Are you okay?" I nodded, though I had no words.

In the days that followed, Rosenwald football practice felt impossibly small and inconsequential, yet some of my teammates practiced as if their very lives depended on every drill. I hadn't joined because I loved the physical toll—though I did love the game's logic from the safety of our living room. On television, football was ordered and contained; up close, at

Rosenwald, it was a desperate, chaotic scramble. I wasn't chasing acceptance anymore—I'd already accepted my status as the "unicorn." Football was about proving something to myself.

Rosenwald was easily the poorest school in Bay County, a living remnant of decades of systemic segregation, and our equipment told the story. Our helmets were antiques with missing padding and broken snaps; we stuffed old socks inside the shells for cushioning. Shoulder pads were held together with literal shoelaces, and the pants barely reached my shins—a cruel joke for a kid with chronic knee problems. My cleats were scavenged from a box in the locker room; I was the only one with a matching pair, repurposed from track after Coach Collier had scoured the county to find them. They were size 13 with plastic spikes worn down to the base metal.

The only thing that looked new was our jersey. We held fundraisers for those who couldn't afford the maroon fabric. Pulling that jersey over my shoulders did something unexpected; wearing number 85 around school on game day provided a sense of pride that is still difficult to articulate. We were playing in the shadow of history—1972 was the year the last two SEC schools finally desegregated their programs. The irony wasn't lost on me: we were running drills together while college programs just miles away were only now opening their doors to kids who looked like us.

A week in, positions were assigned. Coach Templeton put the tallest, skinniest kid in Bay County at defensive end—a decision that made sense only on a chalkboard. I was height without weight, reach without mass. I accepted the assignment without a word. Our first game, on the road against Everitt, turned us into a spectacle. The fans laughed, and even the referees joined in. One ref howled when he saw my braces and my ill-fitting, makeshift uniform. I laughed, too; it was either that or quit on the spot.

We were overmatched. On the first play from scrimmage, a sweep sent me flying, Florida grass lodged in my single-bar helmet. It happened again and again. No one had taught me how to "set the edge"—to force the play back inside toward help. It felt like a stampede of four or five bodies crashing into me with nowhere to go. The coaches responded with public, relentless yelling. Eventually, I reached my limit and yelled back, which earned me the bench for the next game.

Watching from the sidelines, I realized my replacement fared no better. During a timeout, I quietly suggested he line up wider to take away the angle. It worked. The sweep vanished. Practice grew uglier after that, with ridicule replacing actual instruction, until Coach Collier showed up. He watched the dysfunction, shook his head, and asked why the fastest kid in the county was playing defensive end. The next day, I was handed a ten-page playbook and told I was a receiver.

The first slant I ran in practice went for a touchdown. Then another. I felt untouchable until the third attempt, when two defenders arrived at the exact same time as the ball.

The hit landed square in my chest. All the air left my body instantly, like a door being slammed shut inside my ribs. I collapsed, curling instinctively into a ball, my mouth wide open but useless. No sound came out; no breath went in. Panic followed—hot, blinding, and absolute. I lay there gasping, waiting for my body to remember how to function. When air finally rushed back in, it was violent and painful.

Coach Templeton called the same play again. It was a "lesson" because Coach Collier had embarrassed him earlier. I ended the lesson my own way. When the defenders closed in on the next pass, I didn't reach for the ball; I lead with my elbows, catching one in the throat and the other in the nose. Both went down. I slammed my helmet into the turf and walked off. Practice was over.

The next morning, I couldn't breathe. Mom saw me grimacing in the kitchen and pulled up my shirt. "Richard, get in here now." My parents stared at the deep purple bruising set starkly against my dark skin. At the ER, the same nurse from my baseball injury smiled sadly. "You again, sweetie? Don't worry, baby. I'll take care of you."

X-rays confirmed fractured ribs. They wrapped my torso in an Ace bandage and sent me home into the quiet disappointment of my father. That night, I told him I needed to quit. He didn't argue. He just went to bed. But when I walked into my room, there it was on my pillow: the Jackie Robinson book he'd given me in Maine. It was a silent challenge.

Two days later, I was back on the field. I didn't play for two weeks, but I stayed. Our final game was against Port St. Joe—the only game my parents ever attended. I split right, faked inside, and turned back. The ball hit my hands just as my defender slipped. I had thirty yards of open field ahead of me. Through the roar of the crowd, I heard one voice cut through the noise: *"That's my boy!"*

I was tackled five yards short of the end zone, but it didn't matter. We scored on the next play and won our only game of the year. I'd gone from scapegoat to contributor in one play. More importantly, I proved I could endure. A week later, I walked away from football for good—not in anger, but with the clarity that my body and the game were incompatible. I'd finished what I started.

Chapter Thirty-Nine

With my football career relegated to the mothballs of history, I turned to a sport my lean body was actually suited for: basketball. Tryouts were a mere formality; the team had been handpicked to include me because of a single, uncoachable trait: height. At Rosenwald, being the tallest kid in the county made me an immediate asset, a vertical outlier in a sea of guards.

I had everything to learn about the hardwood. I idolized Kareem Abdul-Jabbar; a life-sized poster of him hung in our locker room, frozen in a sky-hook that looked more like poetry than mechanics. I practiced that shot for hours alone in my neighborhood, the rhythmic *thump-swish* of the ball against the backboard becoming the soundtrack of my afternoons. It was quiet, repetitive, devout work. I also became a student of John Wooden's UCLA teams, learning the geometry of the game from the flickering images on our television.

Coach Townsend, a former college guard, filled in the gaps, teaching me the language of the high post and the subtle art of the pivot. He once considered reworking my unorthodox jump shot, but after watching me hit ten in a row from the perimeter during a scrimmage, he wisely left it alone. Before our first game in late January, he named me team captain—not for my raw talent, but for the sheer volume of my effort.

But my body was already sending frantic warnings. One morning, my knee simply buckled before the bus arrived, a sharp reminder that six months of nonstop impact had finally caught up to me. I ignored the doctor's orders for rest; I couldn't bear to disappear again, especially since my parents were coming to see me play for the first and only time.

I iced my knees in secret inside the concrete "cooler room" where the coaches kept Cokes for sale. I was the only student with a key to that damp, chilled sanctuary. My knees were swollen to the size of grapefruits; forty-five minutes on that freezing floor reduced them to the size of tangerines, but left the joints feeling like they were cast in lead. When I led the team onto the court, the truth surfaced instantly: I couldn't jump, and I couldn't pivot without a wince.

Dad noticed the hitch in my gait immediately. His disappointment arrived loudly from the bleachers, fueled by a mixture of alcohol and a jagged, protective fear he didn't know how to express. He shouted criticisms that felt like slurs, his voice sharp and slurred.

Coach Collier eventually crossed the court to try and calm him, speaking in the low, steady tones he used for spooked horses, but Dad wouldn't be moved. Mom and the other coaches eventually intervened, but the air was poisoned. That night, I felt a white-hot, silent urge to punch my own father in the face.

Yet, in the locker room afterward, my teammates closed ranks around me. Their unprompted support made me realize that basketball had given me something football never could: a family that didn't require blood or a shared last name to function.

Then came the game at Carver. We had been told it was a junior high; it turned out to be a high school filled with young men who looked like they'd spent their summers hauling hay. The gym was a cavern of shadows, half the bulbs missing from the rafters, with the only real light reflecting off our six white teammates and our cheerleaders. Carver's starters were as tall as me, their arms thick with muscles and their faces set in a hard, performative bravado designed to intimidate.

Minutes into the game, a Carver player noticed the glint of my dental braces and promised, with a grin to "knock them out of your head." Moments later, a vicious elbow caught me square in the mouth. My mouthpiece flew, and blood splattered onto the hardwood. The officials didn't even whistle. During a timeout, as I was forced to grab a towel and clean up my own blood while the home crowd jeered, a cold, predatory fury took hold of me.

Just before halftime, I saw my opening. I delivered a deliberate right hook to my assailant's jaw. He collapsed like a house of cards. I stood over him, staring down like Ali over Liston, waiting for him to move. I didn't care about the technical foul; I had finally set my own edge.

At halftime, the atmosphere was so volatile that our cheerleaders had to retreat into the boys' locker room for their own safety. Our teammates rallied around us even when the coaches seemed paralyzed by the weight of the moment. The second half was a blur of Black-on-Black vitriol; Carver's coach berated his players with racial slurs I'd never heard before, his voice cracking with desperation because they were struggling against an integrated team. The pressure on them not to lose to "white players" was a physical weight in the room. Paradoxically, after the final buzzer, I was the only person on our roster they would even deign to shake hands with.

We were given a police escort for a mile out of town, the blue lights flashing against the dark pines of the roadside. Only when the sirens faded did the silence on the bus break. I took my usual spot in the back row; my legs stretched into the aisle— a courtesy my teammates extended without question because of the state of my knees. Twelve players and eight cheerleaders huddled in the back of the bus, the air warmer and more intimate than it had ever been.

The conversation that followed changed the way I saw the world. My Black teammates didn't ask *if* places like Carver existed; they knew the map of the South better than I did. They asked if this was the "tax" for crossing lines—for standing alongside of white kids in a world that demanded separation.

They asked us military kids if we'd ever attended a segregated school. None of us had; the Department of Defense schools were an island of integration. But several of the local kids had attended elementary schools that were effectively "separate but equal" in practice, if not in name. For them, Rosenwald wasn't just a school; it was a front line. Integration hadn't arrived like a parade; it had arrived sideways, messy and fraught with a pain I was only beginning to grasp.

We talked about the night Dr. King was killed. I admitted, with a burning sense of shame, that I hadn't even known who he was until the news told me he was dead. No one judged me for my insulation.

They'd lived the nightmare from a different angle. Selma had occurred in 1965, when we were mostly seven-year-olds, but for them, proximity had made the events of "Bloody Sunday" feel like a local tragedy. Their knowledge was an inheritance—passed down through the hushed tones of parents, the warnings of relatives who lived nearby, and the grainy, terrifying images on their televisions. For them, history wasn't in a book; it was the reason their mothers cried uncontrollably, like something inside them had permanently broken.

We rolled back onto campus at ten that night, the engine cut, and we scattered into our parents' cars. Like most of my teammates, I never told my family what had actually happened in that gym. I didn't have the words yet, and I wasn't sure they were mine to share.

Chapter Forty

Basketball ended a week later, following a road trip to DeFuniak Springs—a rural town an hour northwest of Panama City. The school was predominantly white, with a student body of fewer than five hundred, but the reception was the polar opposite of Carver. We were treated like visiting rock stars—met with curiosity and politeness instead of menace. Sitting on the bench late in the game, it finally dawned on me that the season was over.

Young minds don't often think in endings; we assume seasons just roll forward into infinity, that there will always be another practice, another bus ride, another chance to play. But as that final buzzer echoed through the small gym, I understood, without ceremony, that a game I loved had reached its limit.

Before the school year closed, I appeared in a school play. We performed twice—once for the student body and again on a Friday night for the parents. Nearly every seat was filled by white parents who had made the forty-minute drive from Tyndall. In contrast, the parents of my Black classmates were mostly absent, likely tethered to jobs that didn't offer the flexibility of military life. I watched my friends scan the darkened room, searching for familiar faces that never appeared.

To their credit, the white parents did something unexpected. When the curtain closed, they didn't just applaud their own; they embraced everyone. For a brief window of time, kids who wanted nothing more than to be seen were exactly that. It didn't erase the empty seats, but it softened the blow.

I learned early at Rosenwald that lines existed everywhere—some visible, most felt. You were expected to sense and obey them without a map. If you crossed one unknowingly, the consequences arrived swiftly. I had avoided serious discipline by understanding the rules of engagement: keep your head down, be respectful, and be excellent. Until the day those rules stopped working.

I was walking back to class from the nurse's office when I saw a classmate shimmying up a rusted pipe to retrieve a ball from the roof. He was stuck, dangling precariously. Without thinking, I offered my hand to help him down. What should have been a non-event was instantly elevated to "vandalism" by a teacher named Mr. Edison. Context didn't matter. We were escorted to the principal's office like criminals.

Principal Spicer sat behind his desk—calm, compact, and entirely too comfortable in his authority. Judgment was swift: three licks with a wooden paddle. My friend Tim went first; his eyes watered, but he held it together. When it was my turn, something inside me snapped into absolute clarity. There was no universe in which I was pulling down my pants to be paddled by any man, especially a white one. Not here. Not now.

I refused. When they tried to grab my arms, I pushed back with a strength born of pure indignation. Both men stumbled, landing on a sofa in the corner. The room went silent. This wasn't defiance for its own sake; it was history speaking. The symbolism of a white man over two Black boys with a paddle was obscene.

Mr. Spicer threatened to call my father. "Do it," I challenged.

Bull Meechum arrived furious—at the interruption, at the situation, and at the world in general. I braced for the blow, but it never came. Instead, Dad turned his fury on the principal. He made it clear that if punishment was necessary, it would come from him and no one else. Then he looked at me. "Let's go." That single line crossed every other boundary in the room.

The drive home was explosive. The Thunderbird roared through traffic, Dad shouting at anyone who slowed him down.

Eventually, the fire burned out. He asked what really happened, listened, and then did something rare: he apologized. He told me about the nuns at his Catholic school—the beatings, the humiliation, the shame. I finally understood why discipline had always pained him, and why his anger and restraint lived so close together. "You never let another man put his hands on you," he said firmly. "Ever."

The next day, I returned to school. No punishment, no just a dangerous silence that suggested the matter was settled when it wasn't. That same week, Dad told me to walk to my orthodontist appointment—two miles through a neighborhood I'd never navigated alone. I knew the risks but went anyway because Dad told me to.

I didn't make it.

Two men, smelling of alcohol and stale smoke, cornered me in a shaded stretch of the sidewalk. Fear froze me just long enough for them to tackle me to the ground, a blade pressed cold and sharp against the skin of my throat. They took the cash I carried but left the check for the orthodontist behind, a final insult to my dignity. Witnesses walked past on the other side of the street as if I were invisible, or perhaps they were just as afraid as I was. I ran the rest of the way in my dress shoes, my heart hammering against my ribs like a trapped bird.

The nurse at the office saw it all before I could say a word—the blood-stained white shirt, the shallow, stinging nick on my neck, the ripped clothing, and the sweat pouring off me. She called my mother immediately.

That evening, Mom finally found her voice. What followed wasn't just a flare-up of anger; it was a reckoning. She told Dad this place had already asked too much of their son. She told him to stop pretending that "presence" was the same as "protection." She told him, finally, to be the father I actually needed, not the one he imagined himself to be. It was a searing indictment of his drinking, his long absences, and the way I'd been left to fend for myself in a landscape that was clearly hostile. Dad had crossed a final line, and as she stood in that kitchen, Mom was done pretending for the sake of the family. The insulation was gone.

Chapter Forty-One

The night felt ceremonial long before I understood why. The Four Winds Restaurant sat along the marina, its white tablecloths catching the amber glow of overhead lights, silverware aligned with a military precision none of us kids had ever seen outside of television. For most in the room, it was a banquet—an excuse to dress up, eat well, and celebrate the messy, complicated end of junior high.

Students clustered at the back of the room, laughing too loudly to mask their nerves, fidgeting in borrowed jackets and stiff dresses. Parents filled the front tables, many of them strangers to one another, suddenly united by a shared belief that their children had survived something meaningful. My parents sat near the front, stage right, composed and quiet. Mom scanned the room with a practiced eye, while Dad looked restless, his energy keyed up as if he were anticipating a shift in the wind.

To my surprise, Dad was speaking openly and freely with everyone at his table. This was nothing like the icy reception he'd received at the school two years prior. I watched as Principal Spicer and my coaches shared a few laughs with him; it was the first time my parents had met many of my teachers in person.

The podium stood elevated on a small dais draped in maroon and white. Our bulldog mascot—snarling and defiant—stared out at the room like a challenge. Principal Spicer and the coaches took their seats behind it, posture formal, nametags carefully placed. This was Rosenwald dressed in its Sunday best, asserting a sense of dignity in a place where history had often denied it.

Awards followed dinner in predictable waves: Best This, Most Outstanding That. I clapped until my hands stung, genuinely happy for my friends. I even received a few participation awards—basketball captain and top miler—despite the fact that I'd never actually won a race against anyone but my own teammates.

Then the room went quiet.

The final award, they announced, recognized both academic excellence and athletic achievement. Coach Collier spoke first, followed by Principal Spicer. Their words slowed, becoming deliberate and heavy with importance. They described a student who had lettered in three sports despite significant physical limitations. A student who carried a near-perfect grade point average. A student who had arrived at Rosenwald uncertain and was leaving transformed.

Halfway through the description, the room blurred. Before my name was even spoken, I felt gentle hands on my back—pressure and encouragement. I stood on instinct; my legs unsteady and my heart hammering against my ribs. When my name finally landed in the air, the entire room rose with it.

The applause was thunderous and sustained. Teachers, coaches, parents, and students—Black, white, military, and civilian—all dissolved into a single, unified sound. I walked to the podium in a daze. Principal Spicer extended his hand as if our office incident weeks earlier had never occurred. Coach Collier abandoned all formality; he wrapped me in a full-bodied hug and lifted me off the floor, laughing and crying unashamedly.

I shook uncontrollably. I heard a little girl in the front row whisper to her mother, "He's shaking." I looked down and tried to smile, but I was in too much shock to manage even a grin. From the podium, I searched the front row. Mom was crying openly, her face buried against Dad's shoulder. Dad—loud, volatile, complicated Dad—had tears streaming down his face, soaking into the collar of his suit. He gripped Mom's hand like an anchor, a raw pride radiating from him that felt like redemption.

They hadn't known. Even though they had served on the organizing committee, they had been kept in the dark. The trophy was enormous—too large to be held with one hand and heavy with a meaning I couldn't yet articulate. I didn't speak; words would have failed me anyway.

That night wasn't about perfection; it was about survival. Rosenwald had been a proving ground that stripped away my illusions and demanded adaptation. I had arrived naïve and unprepared; I was leaving with scars, wisdom, and something close to peace. We were the first class to complete all three years of court-mandated busing. I still didn't fully grasp my Blackness or how the world saw me, but I understood belonging that was earned, not granted.

The drive home felt unreal. Dad rolled the window of the Thunderbird down at red lights, holding the trophy outside like a declaration, shouting joyfully to strangers who honked in response. For once, his fire wasn't fueled by anger or alcohol, but by a pure, unchecked pride.

Monday came too quickly. Lockers were emptied and books returned. Teachers hugged students longer than necessary, and tears flowed freely. Geography was about to separate us permanently. Most local kids would head to Bay High or Rutherford; we all understood our paths were unlikely to cross again.

Coach Collier waited by my bus and pressed his home phone number into my hand. He made me promise to call him about college—a concept that still felt distant and abstract, but the seed had been planted.

On the ride home, Wilson was unusually quiet. When he finally spoke, his words carried the weight of a prophecy. He told me how much I'd grown—that the scared kid who had boarded his bus three years earlier was gone. He warned me that the world would see me differently now. "Some will recognize the person," he said. "Others will see only skin. Be yourself. God will watch over you."

When the bus doors opened, we embraced one last time. I stepped onto the pavement, turned back, and waved. Wilson was already pulling away. Just like that Rosenwald was behind me.

By the time I left, most of my New England accent had vanished, replaced by a polished, mid-Atlantic cadence that was half-American and half-British, peppered with Southern colloquialisms. It was an accent that would cause confusion for the rest of my life—a voice people couldn't quite put in a box. I had grown to hate labels, realizing that in America, stereotypes are often mistaken for the final truth of a person's existence. I was a man of the world now, and the world was waiting.

Chapter Forty-Two

The Florida State Bowling Championships were held that summer in Pensacola, a hundred miles west of Panama City, where the Gulf of Mexico curves sharply toward the Alabama state line.

Pensacola felt larger, louder, and infinitely more significant than anywhere I'd been in years. Panama City, on a good day, was a sleepy town of under thirty thousand; Pensacola, by contrast, moved with a military purpose. Massive Naval ships crowded its deep-water harbors and fighter jets screamed overhead in a constant, gray-blurred symphony. It felt like a place where history was being made, and for a weekend, I was part of it.

Several teams from Tyndall competed over four consecutive weekends. Because the drive was manageable, most of the older kids rode together—teenagers with fresh licenses, borrowed cars, and just enough freedom to invite the kind of trouble that parents stay awake worrying about.

And we certainly invited it.

Once we reached the hotel, the absence of adult supervision was interpreted as immediate permission. The pool area stayed loud well past the posted curfew, vibrating with the splashes and shouts of kids who felt invincible. When management finally shut the outdoor area down, we retreated inside, ordered pizza, and dragged the night back to our rooms. Florida's drinking age was eighteen then, and several of the older kids tested that boundary with a frantic enthusiasm, sneaking off to local liquor stores and sharing whatever contraband they brought back in brown paper bags.

I didn't drink. I wanted it to look like I had—I spent the night nursing a lukewarm Coke that I claimed was heavily mixed with rum—but the truth was far simpler and more sober. Watching my father's relationship with the bottle over the past few years had made alcohol feel less like a tool for rebellion and more like a visible danger. It was a fire I had no interest in playing with. Dad was also a three-pack-a-day smoker; Mom had managed to quit during our first year in Florida. I'd tried a single cigarette at fourteen, but the acrid taste had disgusted me so thoroughly that I never touched one again. It was one of the few vices of my father's that I successfully avoided.

Sometime around three in the morning, I fell asleep fully clothed, stretched diagonally across the hotel bed. When I drifted awake a few hours later, the room was a chaotic tableau—white kids, boys and girls alike, were scattered across the floor and extra beds in various stages of undress and hungover exhaustion. Bottles were everywhere: the bathroom, the balcony, the shag carpet.

In a sudden, cold panic, I woke everyone up, herding them down the outdoor corridor back to their own rooms like a sheepdog. I cleaned that room as if my very life depended on the shine of the countertops. By the time the sun was fully up, there was no trace of the night's debauchery left behind. I showered, caught a ride with a Black family whose ten-year-old daughter followed me around with the wide-eyed adoration of a younger sister, and headed to the bowling alley to face the lanes.

The warning came a few hours later, delivered without ceremony by Gladys. She approached me quietly, but the look on her face stopped me mid-stride. She stood beside me as I waited for my turn, her eyes fixed straight ahead on the pins.

"Look forward," she whispered. "Don't react to what I'm about to tell you."

She then recounted a conversation she'd had with the hotel manager. "Your party from last night," she began.

I turned toward her, my heart sinking. "My party?"

"Just listen," she said, her gaze never wavering. "I know it wasn't you. But the manager called you every name in the book." She stopped abruptly, her throat tightening, unable or unwilling to voice the specific slur.

I said it for her, the word landing between us like a stone. "He called me the nigger."

She paused for a heartbeat, then nodded once. "Be careful, Michael." And just like that, she walked away, leaving me standing in the middle of a crowded bowling alley feeling suddenly, violently exposed.

I still had another night at that hotel. From that moment on, I never went anywhere alone—not even to the restroom. We moved in defensive groups, taking our fun elsewhere. The beach became our refuge, a vast, open space far from closed doors and the watchful, hateful eyes of hotel managers.

On the lanes, however, the weight of the world seemed to evaporate. I bowled six games that day, and two were well over 200. Spectators began to gather behind my lanes, drawn by scores that didn't match the modest 150 average next to my name. It felt unreal, as if the ball was being guided by something outside of myself. Sunday was more of the same; while our team struggled as a unit, individually, I couldn't seem to miss.

The ride home was a rolling celebration. We ignored the bypass and cruised the beach roads instead, rolling slowly through Destin and Panama City Beach like a low-speed parade. Girls changed into swimsuits in the back of the vans; boys pretended not to stare and failed miserably. Once home, the summer settled into a simple, industrious rhythm: bowling and work, work and bowling.

One afternoon, Gladys sent word through a friend at the commissary for me to stop by the lanes after my shift. When I arrived, a small group had gathered at the far end of the concourse. She took my hand and pulled me forward. They parted to reveal a cake—white icing, a plastic bowling statue in the center. Piped across the top in maroon frosting:

> Michael Bennett State Bowling Champion

The celebration lasted about an hour, but I excused myself early. I ran across the parking lot to the Base Exchange to find my mother, who called my father immediately. The news traveled fast; media requests poured in—a local radio spot followed by a short television appearance. Dad listened to the radio broadcast with rapt, silent attention and watched the television segment from start to finish without saying a word.

Given the recent volatility and the growing distance between us, his response carried more weight than I cared to admit. He praised my composure and my clarity under the hot lights of the studio. He called me "very articulate"—a compliment I accepted with relief, though I wouldn't understand the complicated, backhanded nature of that specific word until much later in life. At the time, simply passing his scrutiny was enough to make me feel whole.

Much later, as our relationship continued to fray, I came to understand the subtext of that moment. Dad had begun to feel a quiet jealousy toward his own son—not out of a desire to see me fail, but out of a deep, unexamined grief. The very opportunities he had worked so hard to provide—by joining the Air Force and anchoring our family within the stability of military life—had illuminated everything he had never known as a child. He saw me receiving the encouragement, the recognition, and the safety that he had been denied. I was the embodiment of his own unfulfilled longings. I wish I had recognized that pain for what it was back then.

Ultimately, what mattered more than the trophies or the titles was the sanctuary the sport provided. Throughout my years at Rosenwald, the lanes were where I went to think, to breathe, and to sort through the emotions I couldn't yet name. When school felt like a battlefield and home felt unpredictable, I went bowling. It didn't save me because I was a champion; it saved me because it gave me a place to stand when the rest of the world kept shifting beneath my feet.

Chapter Forty-Three

After the spring and early summer successes, Florida's humid months seemed to screech to a halt. If not for the persistent shenanigans of the "two Larrys," I might have slept straight through to my sophomore year. They were back to their old tricks—slashing my hours and relegating me to back-room counters where customer contact was non-existent, a quiet reminder of who controlled the space.

Then, an adult bowling friend threw me a lifeline. Having witnessed the Larrys' pettiness, he offered me a job stocking shelves for his vendors—Birds Eye and Minute Maid. The pay was four dollars an hour—a princely sum in 1973—but more importantly, I was paid directly by the vendor. I was effectively untouchable. Between that and my bagging tips, my bank account exploded; during July and August, I was likely out-earning my parents combined.

That summer was also when I met Gabe. We crossed paths in the youth league just weeks before school started. Gabe was an acquired taste; he was loud, narcissistic, and competitive to the point of irritation. Yet, for reasons I never fully grasped, he treated me with a rare, easy kindness. He was white, sharp-witted, and loved basketball as much as I did. When school started, Mom forbade me from riding in his Kelly-green Volkswagen—she never explained why, but I sensed she distrusted the freedom that car represented. Like Joey's family years before, Gabe's parents opened their doors and their refrigerator to me without hesitation. I spent my afternoons at their house, cranking the handle on their ice cream maker and playing cards in a room that felt like a safe harbor.

Rutherford High School, opened in 1961, felt like the penthouse suite of a luxury hotel compared to Rosenwald. The lawns were manicured, the books were new, and the cafeteria food was actually edible. Though only two miles apart, the contrast was a study in scarcity versus abundance. Rutherford was white middle-class suburbia in full bloom. There was no need for forced busing here; geography and the base did the work naturally.

I rode a different bus now—a smaller, blue Air Force transport—but my stop remained directly across from our house. Every morning, I still saw Wilson. Sometimes we exchanged words; usually, it was just a nod. Our friendship endured in those brief, silent acknowledgments. By then, the Bennetts were the neighborhood's longest-tenured residents, and I had become the "it" kid—the State Champion with the local longevity to match.

My grades placed me in honors classes, including a second-period Geometry class taught by Mrs. Brady. She was a rigid Southern woman with a permed crown of hair and an expression set in permanent disapproval. She ran her classroom like a military tribunal. To Mrs. Brady, geometry wasn't about the beauty of shapes; it was about the absolute submission to the rules of the page.

I, however, fell in love with the logic. I spent nights memorizing the SAS (Side-Angle-Side) and ASA (Angle-Side-Angle) Congruence Postulates, fascinated by how three pieces of information could prove the totality of a shape. I mastered the Pythagorean Theorem and began to see the world through the lens of proofs—the "Given," the "Statement," and the "Reason." I understood that if A=B and B=C, then A must equal C by the Transitive Property. It was a world of order that made sense to me.

On the first test, Candy—my study partner—earned an A. I received a D. On the second, I received an F, complete with a red-inked sad face. I knew the logic held; I hadn't just guessed the answers, I had constructed the proofs. I knew my Vertical Angle Theorem from my Corresponding Angles. That night, I retook both exams alone in my room and scored perfectly. That's when I noticed the physical evidence: the erasures on my original papers. Answers had been altered; a "5" turned into a "3," a "Therefore" statement crossed out despite being perfectly logical.

I tested my theory on the next exam by using a pen, essentially forcing a permanent record of my work. I earned a B, but even then, Candy spotted where Mrs. Brady had tried to find "errors" in the margins of my proofs. I confronted her directly, pointing to the Interior Angle Sum Theorem I had cited correctly. She dismissed me with a cold wave of her hand, unable to reconcile the "Given" of my performance with the "Statement" of her prejudice. She had no idea I was actually tutoring half her class, helping them navigate the very proofs she claimed I couldn't understand. When report cards arrived days after my sixteenth birthday, the "F" was there in black and white—the only illogical conclusion in a semester of perfect geometry.

Dad came home early that day, a sign of impending storm. He didn't yell at first. His voice was low and dangerous. When the explosion came, it was fueled by scotch and humiliation. He shattered his glass against the wall. "How dare any son of mine bring home a grade like this," he hissed. He snatched my wallet out of my book pocket in an act of physical violence I'd never seen from him. He ripped my driver's license out of its holder and threw my wallet on the floor.

Two days later, I took it back from his dresser. "You can restrict me from the car," I yelled, standing my ground, "but I paid for this." He raised his hand to strike me, then stopped. His arm fell limp. He turned away in a silence more haunting than any blow.

I showed Mom the evidence of the tampered tests. When she asked why I hadn't come to her sooner, I simply nodded toward Dad, slumped in his recliner. For days, the house felt suspended in amber. Dad couldn't look me in the eye.

That same week, I was practicing with the Rutherford JV basketball team. During a breakaway drill, I rose for my first-ever dunk. I was suspended in the air, confident and clean, when a jealous teammate took my legs out. I hit the floor wrist-first. The crack echoed through the gym. I jumped up, fueled by a white-hot fury, chasing him across the court until the coaches pinned me down.

For the fourth time in three years, I was back in the ER. My arm was set in a cast; basketball and bowling were over. A few days later, Dad came home early again. He didn't shout. He sat in his recliner in the dim light and said, "Grab a chair."

I pulled a kitchen chair directly across from him, bracing for another Jekyll-and-Hyde shift. He stared at the floor for an eternity. "We're being transferred," he finally said.

"Where?"

"The Air Force Academy. Colorado Springs."

The words were a physical blow. Panama City—the bowling alley, Wilson, Gabe, the hard-won peace of Rosenwald—was being ripped away just as it had rooted. He tried to sell me on the mountains and the schools, but I was in shock.

The contrast between this man and the one who had shattered a glass over my geometry grade just days earlier was staggering. There was no alcohol on his breath now, no looming threat of a raised hand. Instead of a procedural announcement at the dinner table with my sisters and Mom, he had chosen to pull me aside first. He offered me a level of respect I hadn't known he possessed—treating me not as a subordinate child to be lectured, but as a partner in the family's next chapter. He sat with me in that heavy silence, allowing the weight of the news to land between us before anyone else knew our life was about to change.

Before I could retreat into my own devastation, he stood and hugged me—the longest embrace I could remember. I didn't cry, but something inside me cracked. I realized that the "permanence" I'd fought so hard to build in Florida was an illusion. I finally understood the silent contract of the military brat: you don't own the ground you stand on; you only own the strength you take with you when you leave.

I knew the military life meant moving. I just never occurred to me it would happen before I finished high school. But the math made sense. We'd been in Panama City four years. While it felt like I was blind-sided, in reality, it was just the natural order of business.

I'd spent the last year with close friends discussing our attendance at many of the Florida colleges—Florida State, just 100 miles away; the University of Florida, down in Gainesville; and Miami. I was a Florida boy through and through. Now it was all gone. I finally understood the silent contract of the military brat: you don't own the ground you stand on; you only own the strength you take with you when you leave.

ACT 3
FULL CIRCLE

Chapter Forty-Four

August 1974

The incandescent glow of the morning sun washed across the windshield as we reached Destin, a beauty so at odds with my mood it felt almost cruel. Temperatures hovered in the upper seventies, a steady breeze rushing through the open windows as Dad guided the station wagon along U.S. Highway 98.

He slowed to let beachgoers cross the road, all of them tan and carefree, headed toward the emerald water with towels draped like capes. After crossing the bridge onto Santa Rosa Island, traffic came to a complete standstill for nearly thirty minutes. The delay felt personal, like one last desperate reminder from the Gulf that Florida wasn't ready to let me go.

Two-foot swells lapped gently against the shoreline, the white sand shimmering as if it were waving a final goodbye. I stared out the window, eyes moist, sitting in quiet disbelief that we were leaving all of this behind for a high-altitude desert I couldn't yet imagine.

We continued through Fort Walton Beach, Mary Esther, and Hurlburt Field—part of the Eglin Air Force Base reservation and the largest Air Force base in the country. Eventually, Dad coaxed the car up to fifty-five miles per hour, only to slow again in Gulf Breeze, where Highway 98 turns sharply north across Pensacola Bay. As the tires hummed over the bridge, the Gulf of Mexico slipped out of view. I watched the horizon until it vanished, a blue world I wouldn't see again for years.

Thirty minutes later, we passed through the tunnel beneath Mobile Bay, emerging near downtown Mobile—the birthplace of Hank Aaron, who earlier that year had broken Babe Ruth's home run record. A few roadside signs marked the achievement, understated but proud in a way that felt like a quiet victory for the South. Outside Mobile, Dad veered northwest toward Hattiesburg, Mississippi, then on toward Jackson. The coastal breeze disappeared almost instantly. Heat and humidity pressed in through the vents, heavy and smelling of pine resin and damp earth. Flags along the roadside hung limp in the stagnant air.

We passed through sleepy southern towns where time seemed to have stalled in the fifties. Rusted cars and trailer parks lined the road, reminders that poverty here didn't bother with neat boundaries. Mississippi looked a lot like Alabama—a green, sweltering blur. Without the state-line sign, you might not have known where one ended and the other began. Dad had learned his lesson about traveling through the deep South from our experience four years earlier. We carried enough food and drink in the wagon to feed a small army. Gas stops were quick and deliberate; he checked the perimeter while the tank filled. He didn't believe in carrying guns, but he believed in the safety of staying alert. We stopped in Jackson just long enough to draw quiet attention—blue and green eyes lingering on Dad a beat too long—but no one approached. He kept us moving.

After nearly four hundred miles of back roads, we finally merged onto a completed stretch of interstate. Dad exhaled a long, audible breath of relief. No more stop-and-go towns. No more guessing which looks mattered and which were just curiosity. Earlier that year, in response to the Arab oil embargo, President Nixon had lowered the national speed limit to fifty-five. Dad, like most drivers with a long road ahead, ignored it. He settled comfortably at sixty-five as we rolled west on freshly paved I-20.

Our next waypoint was Vicksburg, where the highway met the Mississippi River. It was the first southern town I recognized from more than just a road sign. The Siege of Vicksburg had been a turning point in the Civil War—forty-seven days of starvation that handed the Union control of the river. From the bridge, the Mississippi looked enormous and indifferent to the history on its banks. Barges passed in opposite directions with room to spare, American commerce moving steadily on the muddy, churning water.

Once back on the open road, Dad reached for the radio, twisting the dial through a sea of static until voices emerged. That afternoon, the tone of the world changed. President Richard Nixon had resigned. The words landed quietly in the car, but their weight settled in slowly. In a military family, losing your Commander in Chief isn't just a political headline—it's a disruption in the chain of command that feels personal. I broke the silence: "What does that mean for us?" Dad kept his eyes on the white lines of the road. "I'm not sure," he said. After a long pause, he added, "I don't know much about President Ford." No one spoke after that. We just listened to the pundits trying to make sense of the fall of a presidency while we drove deeper into the heart of the country.

We crossed into Louisiana and spent the night in a motel near Shreveport. The next morning, we pushed into Texas. The landscape began to stretch out, the sky growing wider as we bypassed Dallas and stopped for lunch at a nearly empty Denny's in Denton. It was there I saw my first openly gay couple—two women in a corner booth, lost in each other. When they noticed me staring, they didn't scowl; they smiled. I nodded back, a silent acknowledgment of a world that was becoming far more complex than the one I'd left in Panama City.

By one o'clock, I took the wheel for a hundred-and-seventy-five-mile stretch toward Amarillo. Holding the steering wheel steadied me. For the first time, I wasn't just a passenger in my own life; I was moving us forward. Dad yelled only once, when I hesitated between two eighteen-wheelers. "Get your ass moving," he barked. I needed the distraction because the radio was killing me. Every ballad felt like a direct transmission from Dana, my girlfriend back at Rutherford.

She was a petite blonde, a sophomore I'd met in Mrs. Brady's geometry class. We'd been inseparable for six months, passing notes behind the safety of our textbooks. That summer, *Sideshow* by Blue Magic was the anthem of the airwaves. The lyrics—*See the man with the broken heart*—followed me across the state lines like a haunting. Forty years later, that song still reaches inside me. People say smell is the strongest sense tied to memory, but for me, it's always been the music.

Dad resumed driving at nightfall as the landscape shifted to dirt, sagebrush, and tumbleweed. Temperatures climbed past one hundred degrees, and the wind whipped dust across the highway until it swallowed the road. We overshot Amarillo in the dark, but eventually found a steakhouse attached to a country-western bar. The people were kind, and for the first time in days, the tension in Dad's shoulders seemed to drop.

The next day we crossed into New Mexico—the Land of Enchantment—and gained an hour. At Raton, we joined I-25 and caught our first distant view of the southern Rockies. They were jagged and purple, dwarfing the soft Appalachians I remembered from the north. As we climbed toward Raton Pass, my ears popped in the thinning air. Warning signs for falling rock and dangerous crosswinds appeared. Pines replaced cactus. At the summit—7,834 feet—we began the descent into Colorado.

After another 150 miles, Pikes Peak rose into view. It was so sudden and massive it felt like it had been placed there just to intimidate us. It cast a shadow so vast that the city of Colorado Springs seemed to shrink beneath it. Minutes later, Dad turned toward the Air Force Academy.

That night, Karen and I tried to burn off our remaining nervous energy at the hotel pool, still operating on Florida time and Florida expectations. When I opened the heavy exterior door, a blast of mountain air slammed into my chest like a physical weight. It was fifty degrees. The decision was made for us; we retreated back inside, shivering and stunned. I was certain that no one in our family could truly fathom living at this altitude—over 6,000 feet above sea level—where the atmosphere is too thin to hold the day's warmth. Our mid-afternoon temperature had been a blistering ninety-five degrees, yet as soon as the sun dipped behind the peaks, the heat simply evaporated into space. It was a daily variation of forty-five degrees, a thermal rollercoaster that made the steady, humid consistency of the Gulf feel like a lost luxury.

Welcome to Colorado.

Florida refused to loosen its grip. The hotel room was too quiet, leaving too much room for the questions I couldn't answer. When could I go back? What was Gabe doing? Was Dana still crying? I was sixteen, living in the shadow of a mountain, but my heart was still buried in the white sand of the panhandle.

Chapter Forty-Five

The United States Air Force Academy sits at the base of the Rampart Range, its grounds rising from 6,200 to more than 9,000 feet above sea level. On a clear day, you can see twenty miles east across the plains before the earth finally drops away. The view is expansive, humbling, and deceptively calm—a sharp contrast to the crowded, chaotic greenery of the South.

Dad worked at the Department of Defense Medical Examination Review Board—DODMERB—another acronym in a life built on them. It was a prestigious assignment, reserved for the best in the field, and he treated it with a new level of professional intensity. DODMERB reviewed the medical qualifications of every applicant bound for America's service academies. A single mark in the wrong column, a missed heartbeat or a history of asthma, could end a career before it even began.

Dad brought the weight of that responsibility home with him. Thick, beige manuals appeared on the kitchen table, and regulations were studied late into the night under the hum of a single lamp. This wasn't just work; it was the power to gatekeep other people's futures, and he took it with a somber, almost religious dedication.

The geography of the Academy grounds dictated our lives. Three miles from the south gate, the road splits at the base of a mountain. To the north lies Falcon Stadium, the concrete bowl where I eventually sold hot dogs for a season. The pay was abysmal, and the thin air made every stair climb feel like a trek up Everest.

To the west, the road climbs toward the cadet training grounds, dominated by the Cadet Chapel—seventeen aluminum spires, sharp and angular, slicing into the Colorado sky. By day, it is a silver monument to modernism; at night, it stands illuminated against the black void of the mountains like a jagged crown.

Heading south from the fork, the road becomes Pine Drive, looping around the mountain before bending west toward Air Academy High School. It remains the only high school in the country located on the grounds of a military academy. Its mascot is the "Kadet"—a mythical bird meant to be the younger sibling of the Academy's falcons. The school colors were blue and silver, matching the sleek, cold aesthetic of the base itself.

The campus was immaculate. The floors shined with a high-gloss finish, and the lockers were aligned with a military precision that bordered on the obsessive. Everything worked. It looked like a premier institution, but it didn't feel like a school. It had no scars, no layers of history, no whispered stories in the hallways. It was antiseptic—a place where the messiness of being a teenager felt like a violation of the building's code.

At registration, the receptionist greeted me with an enthusiasm that bordered on aggression, her handshake so firm I thought she might yank my shoulder from its socket. My counselor, Mr. Bookman, ushered me into an office stacked high with "organized chaos." He looked over my transcripts, his eyes pausing on the "F" in Geometry from Florida.

"What happened?" he asked, looking over his glasses.

I gave him the short version, omitting the part about the erasures and the prejudice. We both knew the logical conclusion: I'd be taking it again. This time, however, there were no erasures. I sat in that classroom as a sophomore among freshmen, a silent master of theorems and postulates, acing every test with a grim, academic fury. I wasn't just passing; I was proving a point to a woman two thousand miles away who couldn't hear me.

Because the school was overcrowded, the schedule was a fragmented mess. Juniors and seniors started at dawn and left by early afternoon, while sophomores arrived late and stayed until the mountain shadows swallowed the building. There was no lunch hour—only staggered twenty-minute breaks designed to keep the hallways clear and the students moving. On my first break, I bought a juice and a donut from a vending machine—neither of which qualified as actual sustenance—and sat at the end of a concrete picnic table, watching the world go by.

I tried to join conversations. I offered a comment here, a nod there. Each attempt drifted off into the thin air, unanswered. It took longer than it should have to recognize the obvious: I was the only Black student in sight. Two days passed before I spotted another. Then another. Three Black students in a school of nearly eight hundred. By my senior year, I would be the only Black male in my graduating class.

After the rich diversity of Rosenwald and the integrated reality of Rutherford, I wasn't just outnumbered—I was exposed. I stood alone in a landscape that offered no reflection, no cultural reinforcement, and no place to simply disappear into the crowd. Desegregating Air Academy would have required an airplane, not a bus. The only thing whiter than the student body was the perennial snow-capped summit of Pikes Peak looming over the football field.

Weeks passed before I made my first real friend. Kent lived nearby, part of my housing cluster, having just arrived from Hickam Air Force Base in Hawaii. We were misfits for different reasons; I stood out, and he simply didn't blend. We bonded over bowling and the shared grind of part-time jobs. Kent loved engines, a passion I didn't share, but he taught me enough to keep a car running. He rode a Suzuki motorcycle and spared me the long, freezing walk to school—until one icy January morning when we nearly went down pulling out of the lot. I still don't know how we stayed upright on that black ice, but the adrenaline of nearly dying together cemented our bond.

Still, the school reeked of an elitism I couldn't navigate. Most students were the children of high-ranking officers, with cars better than my parents' and stay-at-home mothers who meticulously managed their social calendars. Very few worked. College wasn't a dream; it was a foregone conclusion. I knew immediately that I didn't fit the SAS (Side-Angle-Side) congruence of this place. Everything was misaligned.

I spent my afternoons home alone, suppressing a loneliness that had begun to feel physical, like a dull ache in my chest. I missed Florida with a desperate intensity. I called every friend I had left behind, reaching for familiar voices as proof that my previous life hadn't been a fever dream. When the phone bill arrived, Dad shut the calls down with a clinical finality. I didn't have the language for depression then. I only knew that the silence of the mountains was hollowing me out, and if I didn't find a way to anchor myself, I was going to lose the very person I had fought so hard to become in the Florida sand.

Even at this early stage I'd started mentally preparing myself for the day I could make my own decision and leave. I was less than two years from my eighteenth birthday, and I could start making decisions for myself. As I started to think about that rapidly approaching date with the calendar, everything I thought about my future had vanished in that car ride across the country. I had no idea how to proceed. I had no idea how to support myself.

Chapter Forty-Six

A few days after I met Kent, I made my first real connection at school. Her name was Janice. We sat next to each other in typing class, a room defined by six long horizontal rows of desks where each student was sealed into their own little well of productivity. For the first month, the rhythmic *clack-clack-clack* of the keys was our only communication; we might as well have been on different continents. Then, one afternoon, she leaned over the partition and introduced herself, breaking the mechanical trance of the room.

Janice was a beautiful brunette, about five-six, with a natural athleticism she didn't have to work for. She had a slight pug nose that somehow gave her face a sense of character and mischief. She carried herself with the quiet confidence of someone who knew she was the smartest person in the room but felt no need to prove it. She dressed in the soft sweaters and tailored slacks of the Academy elite, but she never looked "loud." She didn't need much makeup; the mountain air seemed to provide all the color she required.

Our icebreaker was a matter of mechanical superiority. I typed significantly faster on a manual machine than she did on her electric, and with far fewer mistakes. That became our private joke—whispered taunts between timed tests, then elaborate notes passed beneath the desks while the teacher's back was turned. Our hands touched and lingered afraid to pull apart. Soon, we were giggling like children who had successfully pulled off a heist.

Janice and her friend Joan began walking with me between periods, weaving through the crowded hallways of Air Academy. Janice didn't flinch at the stares we drew—and in a school made up of ninety-eight percent white faces, we drew plenty. If anything, she seemed to welcome the friction.

We met during every staggered break, then huddled together after school until her ride arrived to take her back to Douglass Valley, the housing area on the other side of the Academy. Holding hands felt as natural as breathing. The first kiss came one crisp morning on the way to third period, tucked behind a brick pillar. Some kids smiled; most looked away with a chilling neutrality that felt heavier than open hostility.

Three weeks later, Janice asked me to the homecoming dance. I hadn't found the guts to ask her myself—I was still too unsure of my "Kadet" standing and wasn't eager to spend an evening as a social specimen in a tuxedo. Still, when she asked, I said yes without a second of hesitation. Dad bought me a brand-new suit, a sharp charcoal number that made me look older than sixteen. Mom helped pick out a delicate corsage and pressed a hundred dollars into my hand for a "proper" dinner. I even cut my humongous Angela Davis style Afro and styled my hair into a Billy Dee Williams look-a-like. He wore it better. But I tried. I'd never worked so hard to impress a woman in my life.

Two days before the dance, the light went out in Janice. She grew quiet, her eyes avoiding mine in typing class. The next day, she wasn't at her desk. Joan approached me in the hall and handed me a folded scrap of notebook paper.

Dear Michael, I have to cancel our homecoming date. My dad won't let me go with you. Love, Janice.

As I read those words, my mind flashed back to seventh grade in Florida—to the party I'd been uninvited to at the hands of a classmate's father. That was four years ago, but the sting was identical. It proved that I really hadn't dealt with the pain of that first rejection; I simply had buried it under layers of achievement and bowling trophies. Now the wound was ripped open again.

The hard part was sharing this with Mom and Dad. They knew nothing of that Florida incident, so they had no context for why this hit me with such force. When I told them the date was off because of her father's prejudice, Mom felt for me so deeply that she began to cry. In a strange, quiet irony, I wound up consoling her, patting her shoulder and telling her it was okay, even though I was the one with the broken heart.

Dad on the other hand, while it was okay for me to be the shock absorber for his emotional abuse, he sure as hell would never allow anyone else to take advantage of his son. But Dad had no way of retaliating. Her father was a Lt. Col., and Dad, if anything believed in military order. Challenging him to a dual at high noon was out of the question. He stewed for an hour then forgot all about it in his glass of scotch.

The fallout at school was instantaneous. With the "protection" of Janice's presence gone, the vultures moved in. White boys who hadn't spoken a word to me all semester suddenly found their voices. One senior shouted "nigger" at my back in the main hallway; he earned a three-day suspension, but the word stayed in the air long after he left.

On homecoming night, that brand new suite hung in the closet despite Kent's efforts to get me to go stag. What kid shows up at a dance without a date, especially the only Black male in school. I may as well have worn a flashing red sign that said DESPERATE around my neck.

I went to the Air Academy bowling lanes. By then, I was a fixture there with the crew of vets—Chuck, Ed, Art, and the rest. They knew I'd been "kicked to the curb," and they did what military men do: they cracked sharp, well-timed jokes to absorb the impact. I don't remember the jokes, but I do remember laughing so hard tears steaked my cheeks. After the last of their stand-up routines one shouted, "don't send a boy to do a man's job," then patted me on the back.

Shortly after, Chuck slid a plastic cup of beer across the counter—a silent, illegal gesture of solidarity. "Keep your mouth shut," he muttered. "You're a minor, and I'm a dead man if the Air Police see this."

After closing, Chuck sat on the bench and really listened. We'd been on the Academy less than six months, but everyone seemed to know my dad had a thing for the sauce. Chuck offered me a lifeline. He gave me a ride home and told me, "If you need anything—anything at all—you call me." That began a fifteen-year mentorship. He had his own family, a wife and three kids, but he was generally concerned about me.

Dad was often "somewhere else," lost in the DODMERB manuals or the bottom of a glass, and Chuck stepped into that vacuum. He checked my report cards and talked about college as a requirement. At his urging, I repaired my friendship with Janice but kept a disciplined distance. "Take the high road," he told me. "You don't belong in the middle of her family's mess."

But I still ached for a sense of belonging. I turned to basketball, my "last stand." I practiced alone for hours on outdoor courts, sometimes on a thin glaze of black ice, in my winter coat.

Tryouts were a clinical execution of basketball philosophy and fundamentals, the likes of which I'd never experience at Rosenwald or Rutherford. It was painfully obvious how well coached the elite players were. I'd hoped to learn a lot while simultaneously making the team. I was easily the best athlete on the floor, and I knew I was a quick learner.

I told the coaches about my knees, and the trainer wrapped them so tightly I walked like a marionette. During the drills, I was a ghost. No one spoke to me.

After a week of tryouts, the field narrowed by attrition. Several kids simply couldn't handle the grind and quit, leaving thirteen players vying for a twelve-man roster. Then, the thirteenth player quit, too. Mathematically, the path was clear. I had survived the cuts; I was the last man standing. But when the final roster was tacked to the bulletin board, the "math" of Air Academy proved to be as fraudulent as a forged check. One of the quitters—a boy who hadn't even finished the week—was on the list. I had been left off.

I exploded. The rage wasn't just about basketball; it was about the recurring theme of being "erased" to make room for someone else's comfort. It was weeks later before I learned the truth: the "quitter" had pleaded with the coach for a second chance. When the coach initially refused, a parent intervened, leveraging their status at the Academy to secure a spot at the expense of the school's only Black male.

I unloaded on Chuck that night, looking for sympathy, for a witness to the unfairness of it all. But Chuck didn't give me a shoulder to cry on. He looked me dead in the eye and told me to stop feeling sorry for myself. He wasn't being cruel; he was trying to armor me for a world that wouldn't care about my "Proof" of merit. I was too young to see the lesson then. I walked out and didn't speak to him for weeks.

But I didn't stop playing. Most of the players who had made the team were in my P.E. class. Every day, the gym became my laboratory of resentment. I played with an anger so deep it became mathematical. It was a cold, calculated fury that didn't need to shout. My knees, swollen and bound tight in Ace bandages due to the Osgood-Schlatter's, protested every jump shot and defensive slide, but I stayed in the air longer than the pain could reach.

I never picked one of the roster players to be on my team. Not once. I was quiet, never drawing attention to myself, never trash-talking or posturing. I would scan the sidelines and pick the other "misfits"—the kids who weren't supposed to be athletes. Then, I made it a point to beat the roster players every single time.

I played like a man possessed by a ghost. I wanted them to see exactly what they had traded away for a parent's phone call. I wanted the coach, who often watched from the folded bleachers, to see the "non-player" dismantle his hand-picked stars. It was a silent, daily execution. I didn't want their friendship, and I didn't need their acknowledgment. I just wanted the scoreboards to reflect the truth that the bulletin board had tried to hide. By the time the bell rang, I'd be drenched in sweat, my knees throbbing in the mountain chill, but I walked to the locker room with the grim satisfaction of a man who had balanced the equations they tried to break.

I begged Dad to transfer me to a school off base. He refused, telling me to "tough it out." I stopped going to the games and started watching them from the opposing bleachers, hiding in borrowed colors. By December, the fight had drained out of me. Between the social isolation at school and Dad's worsening struggle with alcohol, I reached a state of cold clarity. I stopped caring. The effort required to be "accepted" by the blue and silver elite simply wasn't worth the price of admission.

It was the first time I realized I was truly, fundamentally mentally exhausted. Looking back, I'd inadvertently become the family "Fixer" since the early, tumultuous days in Florida. Despite Dad's domineering personality and his rank, it was often—the teenage son—who held the fragile pieces of the family together. While Mom was the one who enabled our survival in a nurturing, motherly way, she too had begun to suffer emotionally under the weight of the move and Dad's volatility. I noticed the cracks forming in her resolve and stepped into the void whenever I could, acting as a silent buttress.

But the one who paid the highest price was Karen. She and Dad were thick as thieve; she adopted his mannerism and his fiery temperament more than I ever had, or even my little sister. Because I projected an outward appearance of being able to take care of myself, the family focus often bypassed me. Mom was the only person who had even a faint clue about my internal distress, but I made a conscious choice to hide the depth of my loneliness from her. I didn't want to add my burdens to her already overflowing plate.

I was sixteen years old, playing the role of an emotional adult in a house that felt like a tinderbox, and a school that felt like a tomb. I looked at the calendar and did the math. In eighteen months, I'd be gone. I just had to survive the silence until then.

Chapter Forty-Seven

Basketball became a microcosm of Air Academy that crossed over into preparation for my future. I came close to walking away from the school entirely, just to escape the sterile silence of the hallways. Pride stopped me. So did fear. I didn't want to become another statistic of displacement. I didn't want to give anyone the satisfaction of saying, *"See, he couldn't hack the altitude."*

At home, the cold war with Dad continued. College was my argument; enlisting was his verdict. We locked horns like it was a competitive sport—sometimes with quiet, jagged barbs over dinner, sometimes loud enough to freeze the room and send my sisters scurrying to their rooms. In his mind, my path was already decided by the Uniform Code of Military Justice. It never occurred to me during those arguments that I could soon make my own decisions, I just wanted to win; not a recipe for success against a person as stubborn as Richard Bennett, with a mind addled by alcohol.

I listened to my classmates talk about applications, campus visits, and futures fueled by parental encouragement. My own focus narrowed to something smaller and darker: just make it to graduation without breaking.

Academically, I drifted. Of my six classes, only three were even mildly challenging, and none of them engaged my heart. My grades slipped from A's to straight B's—marks earned without opening a single book or scribbling a line of homework.

Detachment, in its own crooked way, became my freedom. The tension etched into my face began to loosen. I caught myself smiling again. No one expected much from me anymore—no one except Chuck.

Bowling filled the space everything else vacated. I wasn't just rolling in junior leagues; I started coaching younger kids and helped run the Special Olympics events. Working with those athletes changed the way I viewed my own "failures." They celebrated a single fallen pin like it was a world championship. Failure didn't humiliate them; it didn't even slow them down. They were just happy to be included in the light.

I was a decent bowler, hovering in the mid-160s, but I wanted the mastery I'd found in Geometry. That's when Pam appeared. She worked days at the lanes and watched me for weeks. On my days off, I'd crawl up a steep dirt path on all fours—two hundred feet of incline—just to reach the bowling center perched above the base. Pam watched me make that climb until she decided I was worth the effort.

She offered to teach me on one condition: I had to listen. Pam was the white version of my mother—steady, witty, and unshakable. A few days after my seventeenth birthday, she went to work on me. She rebuilt my entire physical relationship with the game—my approach, my timing, my release. We did foul-line drills until my arm burned. She taught me to read the "math" of the lane: the oil patterns, the friction, the way a ball enters the pocket at a six-degree angle. Within thirty days, my average jumped twenty pins. I went from an ordinary kid to the best junior bowler at the Academy in a single month.

For the first time since leaving Florida, a question settled in: *Could I do this for real?* On Saturday mornings, I stood glued to the Professional Bowlers Tour on ABC. Earl Anthony—"Big Earl"—was the standard. He made $107,000 in 1975, an astronomical sum that sounded like a king's ransom. I read everything available, treating the words of Dick Weber and Don Johnson like scripture.

At night, I washed dishes at the NCO Club for $1.65 an hour. The raise from my Florida pay felt like genuine progress. Then came the ultimate symbol of independence: a baby-blue 1964 Ford Fairlane. Five hundred dollars, seventy a month.

Freedom came with those keys. I was a 6'4" Black teenager with a burgeoning Afro in a city that was less than two percent African American, driving a blue Ford into rooms where I didn't "belong." But the bowling community treated me with a respect that Air Academy High never could.

That summer, my team competed in the Colorado State Championships in Greeley. It was cattle country; the smell of the meatpacking plant hit you like a physical fist on approach from thirty miles away. Our team won. Two state titles in two different states in three years. I was starting to realize that while I couldn't control where the Air Force sent me, I could control what I mastered once I got there.

Around then, Allison entered my life. She was small, pale, and loud in the best possible ways. She was well aware of her beauty and the effect she had on men, but she was comfortable in her own skin. I resisted her for months—Janice's father had left scars that hadn't quite faded—but Allison eventually confronted me in front of the bowling alley staff. "Are you ever going to ask me out?" We dated for a year, and even after we ended our courtship, her mother kept calling me, inviting me over for hot chocolate or late night moving watching. I'd sit talking with her mom while Allison walked in with a new boyfriend; the awkwardness was always erased by her mother's genuine kindness.

Chuck wasn't pleased with my B-average report card. He kept pushing against Dad's "enlistment" narrative, demanding I look toward college.

We all thought Dad hit rock bottom after word reached us that he was facing disciplinary action for his drinking problem. Instead, it only got worse, enabled by his Army and Navy friend co-workers. The three men would often close the NCO Club and continue long afterward, yet through it all Dad never missed a day of work. I'm guessing he showed up once or twice somewhat inebriated, and that led to the potential punishment. A punishment, that came a few years later with forced retirement.

Dad's problems bent the house around it like a gravitational pull. Mom pleaded with him to get help. When he refused, she contemplated walking out. Our family was in crisis mode with no solution in sight.

I forced myself to stay away for my own sanity. I lived mostly among the adults at the bowling alley, watching the Academy cadets from a distance. I knew the Academy itself was closed to me—my grades weren't high enough and my knees were shot—but those men reminded me of who I had been in Florida: focused and forward-looking.

Pam kept teaching me even when I no longer needed the mechanics. I became a big brother to her daughters, Nicole and Carrie. They trusted me with those girls in a way that felt both radical and sacred. I would take those two little white girls, ages nine and eleven, everywhere—even off the Academy grounds and into the city. In the mid-70s, a tall Black man with two young white girls would have been a lightning rod for trouble in Florida. But here, under Pam's steady gaze, it was just family. The nine-year-old was so attached to me she'd spend half the evening sitting on my lap between frames.

That summer, my old friend Gabe from Panama City moved to the Springs. We roamed Nevada Avenue in my Galaxy, cruising like a scene out of *American Graffiti*. We met girls who tried to ply us with the era's drugs and alcohol, but remarkably, we never touched it. At night, Gabe and I talked about Panama City. The absence still hurt; the hole in my heart from leaving Florida never truly filled. Colorado was beautiful, but to me, it felt culturally empty.

Gabe hated the South; he spat the word "redneck" like it was venom. He protected me fiercely, but he never understood that Florida hadn't broken me—it had forged me. The friendships I built there, across every racial line, had a weight I would never let go of, even today, fifty years later.

Gabe wasn't there for my early years, and he never had to survive busing. The kid with privilege, the son of a colonel, whose family made ice cream every weekend, would never truly understand what I'd survived just to stand on that Florida sand. By the time we met, the rough edges of my childhood had been ground down by the friction of Rosenwald and the Larrys. I was already on my way to being a polished gem—hard, multifaceted, and capable of reflecting the light, even in the thin, cold air of a mountain I never asked to climb.

Chapter Forty-Eight

September 1975

I started senior year reinvigorated, or perhaps just strategically armored. The conversations I'd had over the summer with Air Force Academy cadets stayed with me. Those young men moved through the world with a borrowed certainty—routine, discipline, and a clear North Star. I couldn't join their ranks, but I could mimic their posture. If upward mobility had a doorway for a kid like me, education was the only one left standing.

The Vietnam War ended quietly at the Academy. There were no grand speeches in the dining halls, no folded flags on the evening news that felt different from any other day. Even the veterans I knew—men who had tasted the copper and salt of that jungle—let the moment pass in a heavy, collective silence, as if naming the end out loud might reopen wounds that were only just beginning to scab over.

At school, recruiting posters hung in the counseling offices like high-gloss wallpaper. They were soft sells—scenic vistas, talk of "tradition" and "belonging"—carefully scrubbed of any grit. The country's mood demanded a sanitized version of service. Nobody wanted to talk about body counts or the psychological cost of the "math" Dad dealt with every day at DODMERB. But I knew one thing: if I served, I wanted to be an officer. That meant college.

Chuck had been pushing me toward that truth for months, holding court at the bowling alley with a beer in hand like he was staffing a confession booth. I decided my senior schedule had to change. I had sleepwalked through my junior year registration and signed up for a four-class minimum—a "slacker" schedule that would have been academic suicide for a college applicant. On the first day of school, I made a beeline for the counseling office to add the heavy hitters: chemistry, advanced math, anything with weight.

Overcrowded. Denied.

The bureaucracy of Air Academy was as rigid as the Rampart Range. I was stuck with a hollowed-out day: P.E., biology, library science, and a forgettable elective. By eleven in the morning, I was home, eating peanut butter and jelly sandwiches like a prisoner on a work-release program, watching my brain atrophy while the sun was still high. My counselor, Mr. Bookman, was no help. He treated our "career counseling" sessions like a neighborhood barbershop, wanting to debate the "Thrilla in Manila" or the Steelers' defense rather than discussing my transcripts. He was a master of the "rope-a-dope," dodging my questions about applications until I realized I was entirely on my own.

By October, I realized I was months behind the elite "Kadets" I shared hallways with. I didn't know about deadlines or the SAT/ACT sequence. When I mentioned my frustration to Dad, the fuse hit the powder. We fought with a violence that made the house feel small. I stormed out, slamming a glass door with such fury that it shattered into a thousand jagged diamonds. I stood there, chest heaving, staring at the debris. It was a perfect metaphor for our relationship: transparent, fragile, and now, dangerous.

I scheduled another appointment with Bookman. He gave me nothing. So, I went to the library.

Every day, two hours a day for two weeks, I sat among quiet shelves and tried to reverse-engineer a system nobody had ever taught me. I didn't know how people got into college. Choosing a major was the easy part. I'd always wanted to be a play-by-play announcer—if not a military officer. I'd never seen a Black announcer. Maybe I could be the first.

I hunted journalism programs like a man searching for water. USC. Illinois. Columbia. Arizona State. Each one required an SAT or ACT score, so I aimed there first.

I took the ACT in late October, paying for it with my own dishwashing money. I told Mom; I didn't tell Dad. I bombed. Not because I lacked the intellect, but because I didn't know the "game." I didn't know about test-prep or the specific logic of standardized traps. I walked out humbled, Dad's "I told you so" voice echoing in my head. But the competitive instinct that had won me state bowling titles woke up. I registered for the February SAT, studied until the words blurred, and performed exceedingly well. I restored my belief that I belonged in the room, even if the room was empty.

Reality, however, had one more punch. I'd missed the fall application deadlines for the major universities. I didn't understand the "hidden" language of higher education: grants, scholarships, out-of-state tuition. It hit me then that dad's push toward enlistment might not have been just about control—it might have been about shame. We didn't have the money for a four-year university, and his pride wouldn't let him admit it. I pivoted to junior college—affordable, local, and honest.

* * *

Bowling picked up right where it left off—only sharper. My average climbed into the 190s. In the youth circuit around the Springs, my name started circulating like a rumor. On January 18, 1976—ten days after my eighteenth birthday—the *Gazette Telegraph* ran the headline:

"18-Year-Old Rolls Top 695 Series."

Games of 229, 211, and 255.

At the time it was the second-highest series in the history of the American Junior Bowling Congress - Pikes Peak region.

I thought again about going pro. I'd never seen a Black bowler on the televised portion of the PBA tour—just like I'd never seen a Black sports play-by-play announcer. I wanted to be first at something. I wanted my presence to mean more than exception.

Years later I would learn about Fuller Gordy—Berry Gordy of Motown fames older brother—who bowled professionally in the early 1960s. Back then I didn't know the name. Even if I had, the truth would've stayed the same: professional bowling required sponsorship, travel, money. And the paydays weren't what people imagined. Only a small percentage made a living. I kept bowling anyway.

That winter brought the bizarre saga of Mrs. Johnson and her daughter, Cybil. Mrs. Johnson would sit at my scoring station during my practice sessions for hours, delivering baked goods and "selling" her daughter to me with an aggressive persistence I didn't understand. I eventually took Cybil on a date, and we began a year-long relationship that felt like a fugitive operation. Mrs. Johnson would deliver Cybil to me at the bowling alley like a hand-off in a spy novel, eventually confessing that her husband—a man from Alabama—despised Black people. I was living a double life: a celebrated athlete on the base and a "threat" to be hidden around the corner of a residential street.

Then, with a month left of high school, the floor fell out. It started with an act of perceived helpfulness on the side of a mountain road. I stopped to help two classmates whose car had stalled. In the course of the conversation, they offered to sell me a cassette player. I didn't have the money on me, but they let me put it in the trunk planning to settle the debt later. When I showed it to Kent a few days later, his face went pale. He recognized it immediately as a friend's stolen property.

Dad showed up at school without warning and had me report to the front office. I could tell he was beyond pissed, though I had no idea what the trigger was. He didn't offer a greeting. He just looked at me with eyes like flint and said, "Not a word." Then: "Take me to your car."

I led him to the parking lot in a daze of confusion. "Open the trunk," he commanded. I complied, swinging the lid open to reveal nothing but the spare tire and a few stray school papers. He stared into the empty space, slammed the trunk shut.

"Go home" was the next command. "NOW!"

We arrived at the house, when the storm broke, but it wasn't the kind that clears the air. Dad proceeded to tear apart my room—the closet, the dressers, my desk, under my bed, even flipping the mattress. He looked at me and said, "where is it.?" I still had no idea what he was talking about. "Did you steal someone's cassette player?"

"No. I was actually getting ready to buy it." "I showed Kent, and he recognized it belonged to his friends, so I gave it to him, to give back to his friend."

"Then why are the police calling me?"

The drive to the station was a silent, suffocating blur. In the military, a dependent's trouble is the sponsor's summons, and Dad took the summons as a personal stain on his rank. The station sat right next to his office; he knew these detectives by sight, which only deepened his shame. They made him sit in the hall—a move that clearly grated on his sense of control—and took me into a room that looked more like a corporate conference center than an interrogation room.

The two detectives, Master Sergeants Davis and McIntosh, were professional and measured. They turned on a tape recorder and announced the coordinates of my life: *April 1976, 1:00 p.m. Interviewing Michael Bennett regarding stolen property.*

I remained calm. Since Dad had inadvertently tipped their hand, I knew I hadn't committed a crime. They began asking about a string of electronics thefts across the Academy. I soon realized that Kent hadn't returned the deck to his friend; he had turned it into the police. When they showed me a photo, I confirmed it was the same one I'd handed over.

Then came the sucker punch. The two boys, looking for a way out of a mounting list of felonies, had pinned the entire operation, whatever that was, on me. They had branded me the "Black Mastermind."

"ME?" I asked. The tone of offense in my voice was so sharp it actually caught the detectives off guard.

The questioning continued for about thirty minutes. They showed me more photos of recovered loot. In a strange twist of irony, one of the photos was of my own eight-track player that had been stolen out of my car while I was working a night shift at the NCO Club a month earlier. The detectives seemed almost amused—here was the "mastermind," a victim of the very ring he was accused of leading.

At the end, they laid out a spread of photos. I identified the two boys immediately. It turned out the police had been watching them for months—a fact they neglected to tell Dad. As I was being released, Davis looked at me and said, "We might need you to testify."

"Sure," I said, and walked out.

On the ride home, I gave Dad the "Cliff Notes" version, but he wasn't interested in the truth. He didn't defend me; he interrogated me. When we hit the front door, he exploded at Mom, calling me a criminal and accusing me of everything from armed robbery to the Manson murders. It was as if every A-grade, every bowling trophy, and every act of responsibility I'd shown over the years had been erased by a single lie told by two boys trying to save their own skins.

Two days later, the detectives called again. Dad insisted on driving me, convinced I was still hiding something. I went in alone and was out in less than ten minutes. The boys had been arrested. They had pleaded guilty through their fathers/sponsor who, I was told, threatened their sons with more "discipline" than the law ever could. Detective Davis walked out, shook Dad's hand, and thanked us for our cooperation.

It should have been over. The police blotter hit the local paper, the facts were public, and my name was clear. But for Dad, the acquittal didn't matter. He simply could not accept that I was innocent.

Dad didn't show up for my Baccalaureate at the Cadet Chapel. He didn't show up for my graduation the next night. He spent the evening drinking at the NCO Club, choosing the company of a glass over the sight of his son in a cap and gown.

On graduation night, we were lined up in a concrete underground stairwell, arranged alphabetically. I was near the top of the stairs, looking down at a sea of hundreds of white faces—laughing, buzzing, vibrating with the expectation of a world that was designed for them. I stood there, the only Black face, and wept quietly into the polyester of my gown. My grief wasn't just about the investigation or Dad's empty seat; it was the crushing weight of being the "exception." Every success I had felt like a temporary reprieve; every false accusation felt like a permanent sentence.

I pushed thoughts of my recent appearance before the police to Rutherford High School, in Panama City. How many of my friends would be celebrating, what to this point in our young lives was a monumental achievement? I wanted to scream. I didn't belong here. This was the wrong graduation.

Mom, Karen, and Mandi took pictures of me for what seemed like an eternity. The few friends I had walked up and congratulated me, mom beaming with pride. With that it was all over.

There were no house party invitations for me that night. While my classmates were being poured drinks by their parents in Douglass Valley, Rock Rimmon, and other neighborhoods at the Academy or off-Academy grounds, I sat on Kent's front doorstep, wrapped in a blanket, drinking cheap wine until the sun came up over the mountains.

As I looked back over the arc of Spain to Maine, Florida to Colorado, I realized my childhood hadn't been a journey. It had been a series of proofs. *Given:* A world of exclusion. *Statement:* I will excel anyway. *Reason:* Because the only other option is to vanish.

EPILOGUE

My obsession with college didn't fade after graduation—it detonated. I turned Dad's disapproval into fuel and used the sterile isolation of Air Academy as a blueprint of exactly what I refused to become. I carried a chip on my shoulder sharp enough to cut glass; I had allowed too many outside voices to dictate my ceiling for too long, and I was done listening.

Pikes Peak Community College became my first real doorway. It wasn't a consolation prize; it was a tactical gateway. To fund it, I took a second job as a gas station attendant at the Academy AAFES station and began stockpiling money the way other kids stockpiled dreams. Every extra dollar had a hard-coded destination: tuition, books, and the four-year university that would eventually provide my exit ramp.

I built my life on a spreadsheet. Study hours were blocked out on paper with military precision. Work blocks were immovable. I treated civilian college like a high-stakes mission, borrowing the "posture" of the cadets I saw every day. Within two months, I'd saved enough for a full year of tuition. A few months later, year two was covered. The job was mindless, which was its greatest asset; it freed my mind to wander. I studied at the counter between customers, propping my textbooks behind the outdoor island register.

There were two types of people who disrupted that rhythm: the "high society" officers' wives who looked through me as if I were a mechanical extension of the pump, and the chronically lazy who resented my efficiency. I kept bowling, too—adult leagues now—whenever I wasn't pumping gas, washing dishes at the NCO Club, or buried in a book. I didn't want comfort; I wanted momentum. I lived on a diet of adrenaline and caffeine, sleeping just enough to avoid a total physical collapse.

Then Dad called me home, and the "Fixer" finally ran out of tape.

He was furious about two things. First, he was tired of paying my car insurance. That was an easy fix; I had the cash and secured my own policy within forty-eight hours. The second cut was deeper. When he realized I had been putting myself through school at Pikes Peak—on my own dime and my own terms—his fury shifted into something sharper. He let me outline my plan for a few minutes, just long enough to make me believe he might finally see me. Then, he cut me off mid-sentence, calling me a fool for "wasting time" on a junior college degree.

The argument that followed was the loudest of our lives. F-bombs served as punctuation. I walked out into the thin mountain air and didn't look back. That night, I rented a hotel room and stared at the popcorn ceiling, realizing for the first time that I hadn't budgeted for the cost of independence. I hadn't budgeted for rent. To survive, I had to withdraw from school for a semester, watching my hard-earned savings evaporate into the basic necessities of food and shelter.

Mom tried to bridge the rift, but the tectonic plates had shifted too far. Dad and I didn't speak for nearly two years—with one haunting exception. Two months after I moved out, he showed up at the gas station in full uniform. His stature was there, but the man inside was crumbling.

"Your mother left me," he said.

I wanted to be sympathetic, but all I felt was a bone-deep exhaustion. I had been the silent witness to their erosion for a decade. Still, I reached for the version of him I loved—the man he'd been before the ghosts of Vietnam took up residence in his head. I put my arms around him, and he cried—openly, desperately—standing in front of his eighteen-year-old son and a line of confused customers. Alcoholism and untreated PTSD were finally collecting their debt, and the price was his marriage.

Mom had already told me earlier that day. She didn't need to explain why; I knew the "why" better than anyone. I offered her what little money I had left, but she refused, telling me to protect my own future. That was Mom—steady and selfless, even while her world was in pieces.

By Christmas 1976, the family was fractured. Dad spent the holidays in a bottle, and I found myself in the role of the guardian, trying to talk a Senior Master Sergeant into AA. It was a role reversal that felt like a lead weight. Then, the cold moved in.

That winter was brutal—highs in the teens and wind chills that bit through layers of thermal gear. I worked the gas station in an unheated booth, my fingers so stiff I could barely count change. One afternoon, while helping Mom with a low tire at the station, my manager—a woman who had been hoarding racial epithets like ammunition—finally let them fly. She cursed me out in front of my mother. I fired back with two years of suppressed rage and walked out. I was fired the next morning. I fought for my job and won a temporary reinstatement, but the manager cut my hours to a single day a week. It was a "soft fire." I quit.

I took a night janitor job at a bank, scrubbing toilets for two hours a night. It wasn't enough. I applied everywhere. One sporting goods store put me through an inkblot test and a lie detector for a minimum-wage position. They told me I passed. They never called. To this day I still don't think that was a legitimate job. The place where I took the lie detector test was an unmarked building in downtown Colorado Springs. The building only had a table, two chairs, and a suitcase full of equipment. I think they were testing their new technology, and

I was a guinea pig. I called the store one day to follow up. 'We don't have an openings."

The message was finally clear: Colorado Springs was a dead end.

In March 1977, I packed my baby-blue Ford and headed back to the only place that ever felt like home. The drive was a mirror of the one we'd taken years before, but this time, I was the one at the wheel. I stayed with Mom one last night in her new townhome. We ate breakfast in a silence that was heavy with the things we couldn't fix. When I finally crossed into Texas, the tears hit me so hard I had to pull over. I called her from a payphone, both of us sobbing across the miles.

I drove forty-eight hours straight. South of Hattiesburg, I fell asleep at seventy miles per hour. An eighteen-wheeler's air horn ripped me back to reality just as I was drifting into the median. I missed death by inches. I pulled over, soaked in a cold sweat, my heart hammering against my ribs.

When I finally rolled into Panama City, the "homecoming" lasted exactly three days. Then, the "Do Not Hire" code from Colorado caught up with me. The manager from the Academy gas station had blacklisted me in the AAFES system. I'd already worked at the Tyndall AFB gas station for three weeks. The manager there was glad to have me, someone he wouldn't have to train. Despite my glowing record at Tyndall, I was reluctantly terminated after everyone in command at Tyndall tried to get AAFES to act. Then, my old nemesis at the bowling alley finished the job, calling security and claiming I was no longer a military dependent. Dad, lost in a relapse, refused to vouch for me.

My enrollment at Gulf Coast Community College and my dreams of immediate higher education crushed in less than 48 hours.

By August 1977, the "polished gem" was homeless.

I slept in my Galaxy, often in the hospital parking lot where Dad worked when he was station there, because it was the only place that felt "safe." I kept my clothes in a milk crate in the trunk. I learned the "geometry" of a car seat—how to wedge my 6'4" frame into a space meant for a passenger. I washed my face in the sinks of hospital bathrooms, moving quickly so no one would see the "Kadet" who had fallen from grace. Duct tape held my shoes together.

Hunger became a calculation. Do I buy a gallon of gas so I can get to a potential lawn-mowing job, or do I buy a loaf of bread? Usually, gas won. In November, a motorcycle smashed into my car, shattering the rider's knees. It wasn't my fault, but I couldn't afford the deductible. I lived in the rental car Mom helped me get, a transient in a city I used to own.

I had fallen as far as the earth would let me.

One night, I slept on the beach, the sand a cold, damp reminder of my childhood. I woke up in the dark to a three-foot black snake coiled around my foot, searching for the heat of my body. I didn't scream; I just shook my leg until it slid off into the dunes. That was the moment of clarity. I wasn't a "Fixer" anymore. I was just a ghost.

On November 10, 1977, I walked into a recruiter's office broke and starving. I took the ASVAB. I didn't want the military, but I needed a floor that wouldn't drop out from under me. Three days later, I was sworn in. I spent four more months homeless, waiting for my ship date, mowing lawns and doing odd jobs just to eat.

The "polished gem" had been through the fire. Now, it was time to see if it would break or shine.

March arrived with a biting, indecisive wind. Dad and I were talking again—sober this time. He'd returned to the rooms of AA, and he and Mom had begun the fragile, grueling process of reconciliation. I needed a place to leave my baby-blue Ford

Galaxy before shipping out for basic training, so I prepared for one last cross-country haul back to Colorado.

I left Panama City at 3:00 a.m. with exactly forty-two dollars and two peanut butter-and-jelly sandwiches wrapped in wax paper. I pulled off at a rest stop in Mississippi exhausted. I grabbed the baseball bat under my seat, locked the doors and went to sleep. A few hours later I woke to find a Mississippi Highway Patrol officer sitting behind me in his car. We each got out of our vehicles. He offered a hearty handshake. He was easily the largest human being I'd ever seen until I meet Shaquille O'Neal in 2012 on the day Dad passed away from pancreatic cancer. "I've been sitting here watching you for a few hours. I had to chase off a couple of boys about to ruin your day." I was stunned and scared. We discussed my pending entry into the Air Force and exchanged other pleasantries as I drank a Coke he'd retrieved from his car. I never stopped again.

By the time I hit the Colorado border, the math was terrifying: I had twenty-five cents, a quarter tank of gas, and 150 miles of terrain left to negotiate.

I began a desperate dance with physics. I would accelerate to seventy-five miles per hour on the flats, then cut the engine entirely on the downgrades. I sat in the sudden, eerie silence of the car, listening to the wind whistle through the door seals and the rhythmic *thrum-thrum* of the tires on the asphalt. The car was like a ghost coasting through the Rockies, restarting the engine only when my speed bled away to forty. Each turn of the key felt like a prayer; each sputter of the carburetor felt like a judgment.

I ran out of gas on the street right in front of my parents' brand-new Bunkhouse Drive home. The engine coughed once, shuddered, and died with a finality that brought tears to my eyes. I sat there in the silence of my hands still gripped tight on the steering wheel. I'd made it.

I jumped out of the car to stretch my legs when a neighbor approached. "Hi I'm Nadine. You must be Michael." We'd never met but my parents told her I'd be coming. "I prepared something for you to eat." I started to politely decline, but truth be told, I was starving.

Dad made it home first. He hugged me like he actually meant it. I was glad he'd found sobriety, but the anger remained, a cold stone in the pit of my stomach. I couldn't escape the feeling that his choices forced my detours—that his refusal to see my potential had cost me a year of my life. In the end, his "enlistment" path had won, and that was the weight I knew I would carry into the barracks at bootcamp.

On March 28, I flew to San Antonio and boarded a bus to Lackland. The military gave me exactly what I needed: a reset. My anger at Dad fuel me during those early years, but I knew deep down I'd need to let go. I couldn't let him live rent free in my head. Assistance came in the form of an old friend.

After basic and technical school, I landed back at Tyndall, for the third time. Within a week I ran into Coach Collier—now Director of Education on base. He'd earned his own master's degree in the years that followed Rosenwald.

Finally, someone who believed in me. We spent several hours distilling what happened to me since junior high. Our discussion left him speechless. I'd easily been the most promising student he ever had. After I wiped a few tears, he helped me re-enroll at Gulf Coast Community college, the very school I was forced to abandon a year earlier; when I lost my job and my old bowling alley nemesis turned me into the police for no longer being a dependent. This time my tuition would be paid for by Uncle Sam.

After nearly eight years on active duty, and two assignments, I had not completed two years of college. Evening classes, transfers, TDY (temporary duty), and my Air Force job as a computer systems analyst constantly interfered with my attendance. By my calculation I was eight to ten years behind where I should have been had I gone to college like I originally planned.

If I had to be honest with myself, being in the Air Force felt stagnant, like a hamster on a wheel. There were very few challenges, if any, that I felt contributed to my growth. Then burnout set it. I needed a challenge. I left the military at age 28 to focus fulltime on my studies, and at the ripe old age of 35, I finally earned my Bachelor of Arts degree. It was a mixture of exhilaration and relief. The only thing that made me happier than my life-long pursuit of knowledge was the birth of my son, who turned seven the year I graduated.

SURVIVAL.

ADDENDUM

I grew up Black in America—but not where most people expect that story to begin.

My childhood unfolded inside military installations scattered across the United States and abroad. These were self-contained worlds: guarded, regulated, and insulated. Places where families lived behind gates, where rules were posted at the entrances, and where daily life operated under a version of the Constitution reinforced by military law.

As a child, I didn't understand any of that. It simply felt normal.

Inside those walls, race functioned differently. Not perfectly. Not without friction. But differently enough to distort my sense of the country beyond them. Housing wasn't segregated. Schools were integrated by default. Neighbors were assigned by rank and need, not by skin color. Black, white, Latino, Asian, Jewish—everyone lived close enough that difference became background noise rather than a defining feature.

That environment didn't erase race. But it delayed its meaning.

That wasn't accidental history.

What makes my experience unusual—even among military dependents—is not the movement itself, but *where* I landed at key moments in American history.

Military families move constantly. That part of the story is common. What isn't is repeatedly living in civilian-adjacent environments, during the 1960s and 1970s, where there were so few people who looked like me. That absence mattered.

In theory, military life was designed to counter segregation. In practice, outcomes varied widely depending on location, timing, and proximity to the civilian world beyond the gates.

Many military brats grew up in visibly integrated base communities that mirrored—or even surpassed—the diversity the country claimed to be working toward.

I didn't.

At critical junctures—Florida in the early 1970s, Colorado in the mid-1970s—I found myself in environments where integration existed on paper but not in daily experience. Schools, neighborhoods, and social circles that were overwhelmingly white, with few cultural counterweights and even fewer guideposts.

Those were years when exposure might have mattered most. Years when the country was wrestling publicly with race, identity, and belonging—while I was absorbing none of the context that struggle produced.

This wasn't a typical military upbringing. It was a narrow one. Not by design, not by intent—but by circumstance layered upon circumstance.

By the time I arrived in that world, it was already normalized.

Outside the gates, America was fighting itself—over civil rights, over schools, over who belonged where. Inside, those battles were muted or invisible. The noise of history was reduced to static. We heard echoes, not alarms.

While the country convulsed through assassinations, protests, riots, and legislation, I was somewhere else—geographically and psychologically. When history reached for me, it often missed.

I didn't witness the Civil Rights Movement as it unfolded. I didn't march. I didn't protest. I didn't absorb the language of Black resistance or the vocabulary of survival that so many of my peers carried instinctively. I wasn't taught those things at home either—not out of neglect, but out of circumstance, silence, and exhaustion.

What I absorbed instead was a kind of provisional belonging.

That illusion held—until it didn't.

Each time we moved off base and into the civilian world, the contrast sharpened. The rules changed without warning. My body began to mean something I hadn't been trained to interpret. Expectations shifted. Signals appeared that I couldn't read. I was enrolled in a course I hadn't taken the prerequisites for.

Race 101. No syllabus. No instructor. Just consequences.

By the time I entered spaces where I was suddenly *the only one*, the insulation was gone. What had once felt like neutrality was revealed as absence. What I lacked wasn't intelligence or resilience—it was context.

That gap shaped everything that followed.

It explains my naïveté. My misreads. My confidence in rooms that didn't want me. My confusion in rooms that did.

It explains how a childhood of relative stability could give way, abruptly and brutally, to dislocation. How someone raised with structure could fall so far, so fast—without understanding why.

This addendum isn't here to excuse that journey. It's here to locate it.

I didn't grow up outside American history. I grew up just far enough from it to miss the lessons everyone assumed I knew.

This book isn't an argument. It isn't a diagnosis. And it isn't a solution.

It's a record of what happens when identity is postponed, when belonging is conditional, and when a child is raised *elsewhere*—geographically, culturally, historically—then released into a country that expects fluency without instruction.

If the story resonates, it's not because my experience is unique. It's because versions of it still exist—quietly, systemically, just out of frame.

ACKNOWLEDGEMENTS

This book exists because a few people shaped my life in ways that mattered—some through presence, others through sacrifice, and some through belief when belief was hard to come by.

To Cecilia Walters, known to me as Boo—thank you for your steadiness, patience, and unwavering belief. Your encouragement gave me the courage to return to this story with honesty and clarity. I remain deeply grateful for your presence in my life.

To my son, Michael David—watching you become the man you are today, and the father you've grown into, has been one of my life's greatest privileges. I am endlessly proud of you. And to your children—Kayra, Mariah, Xander, Anton, and Michael Romeo—it has been the joy of my life to share a home with you and watch you grow every day. You keep me young in ways I never expected, and you remind me daily of what truly matters.

To my daughter-in-law, LeoVictoria—the warmth, compassion, and kindness I see in these children are a direct reflection of you. Thank you for the love you pour into your family and for the grace you bring into our lives.

To my father, Richard. He passed away in 2011, but his impact on my life is undeniable. The single most consequential decision he ever made was joining the United States Air Force just months after I was born. That choice shaped the trajectory of my life in ways I am still coming to understand. While our relationship was complicated and marked by struggle, I recognize and appreciate the sacrifices he made and the doors his service opened for me. I carry both the lessons and the gratitude forward.

Finally, to my mother, Anita. She passed away in 2021 after a long battle with Alzheimer's, but her love, strength, and belief remain indelible. She gave me permission to dream when others did not. She encouraged curiosity, resilience, and hope. This book—and the life behind it—rests on the foundation she built.

ABOUT THE AUTHOR

Michael Gordon Bennett is a writer, producer, and storyteller whose work explores identity, displacement, and the quiet ways history shapes individual lives.

Born into a military family, Bennett spent his childhood moving between the United States and overseas assignments, growing up in environments that often insulated him from the broader social and racial realities unfolding elsewhere in America. Those formative experiences—living on military bases, attending integrated schools, and navigating predominantly white spaces during pivotal moments in U.S. history—form the foundation of *Out of Frame*.

After a winding path that included military service, periods of instability, and a long pursuit of higher education, Bennett earned his bachelor's degree from California State University, Northridge. He later completed a Feature Film Screenwriting Certificate through University of California, Los Angeles, further refining his narrative approach and cinematic sensibility.

Bennett has worked across film, television, and independent media, developing character-driven stories rooted in lived experience. He is the founder of 727 Squared Entertainment, where he develops narrative projects across publishing and film, and the founder of the T.R.U.T.H. Initiative, a nonprofit organization dedicated to uncovering, preserving, and amplifying overlooked histories through storytelling, education, and cultural engagement.

He lives with his family and is the proud father of one son and the grateful grandfather of five—Kayra, Mariah, Xander, Anton, and Michael Romeo—who continue to remind him that perspective, humor, and curiosity are essential survival skills.

For more information, visit — https://727squaredent.com

THIS PAGE INTENTIONALLY LEFT BLANK

www.ingramcontent.com/pod-product-compliance
Lightning Source LLC
Chambersburg PA
CBHW032035290426
44110CB00012B/815